ISBN: 0-9821196-8-2
ISBN 13: 978-0-9821196-8-6

Y0-DFK-722

You can visit us online at: *www.JacKrisPublishing.com*

Printed in the United States of America.

Ver. 1.0.0-1

<u>Preface</u>

We have designed this thorough program to be user friendly for both teacher and student. The Level 1 program consists of this workbook and the **Teacher's Notes/Answer key**.

At the beginning of the workbook is a table of contents that lists the concepts and the lessons that pertain to each.

We have selected spiral binding for our books to ensure that they lie flat when open. The spiral binding at the top of the page provides equal, unobstructed access for both right and left-handed students.

Thank you for choosing *Soaring with Spelling*. We look forward to the opportunity to provide you with the best tools possible to educate your children.

How To Use This Program

This program is arranged in 36 weekly lessons. Each lesson consists of five exercises labeled **Day 1** through **Day 5**.

For the level 1 program we have selected six list words for each week (for each lesson). Six new words each week should provide an adequate challenge for a student at this level. The list words are meant to provide the student with an introduction to one new spelling concept each week. By gently introducing each new concept, one at a time, the student should not become overwhelmed.

We have found that most children in the age group for which these materials are designed usually need to spend about 10-15 minutes per day on spelling and vocabulary. If your student happens to progress through the material at a faster rate, you may want to consider condensing each lesson into a four day schedule. This can be accomplished in a number of ways, such as combining **Day 1** and **Day 2**, or perhaps combining **Day 4** and **Day 5**. It's really up to you as long as all of the materials are covered during each week.

Please see the **Teacher's Notes/Answer Key** for a detailed explanation (which includes a recommended **Weekly Schedule**) on how to use these materials.

Level 1

Table of Contents

Student's Name: _____

Soaring with Spelling and Vocabulary

Level 1

<<The page intentionally left blank.>>

Lesson 1
Day 1

| Words with short vowel **a** sound |

1. **Review Your Word List**
   Look at the word list below and read each word to yourself. Then review each definition.

List Words

| sat |
| hat |
| and |
| sand |
| can |
| fan |

Definitions

- To rest upon a portion of the body where the hips and legs join.

- A covering for the head.

- As well as, also, to add.

- Small granules made of broken rock. To make smooth.

- A cylinder shaped device made of metal.

- A device which moves air.

2. **Take Your Pretest**
   Turn to the next page to the Pretest section and your teacher will ask you to write each list word one at a time.

Pretest - Lesson 1:   Correction Area:

1.

2.

3.

4.

5.

6.

Lesson 1
Day 2

sat	and	can
hat	sand	fan

A. Find the list words that rhyme. Draw a line to connect each pair.

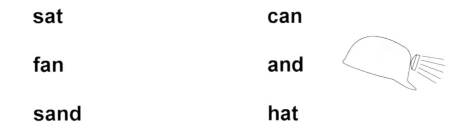

sat   **can**

fan   **and**

sand   **hat**

B. Complete the list words.

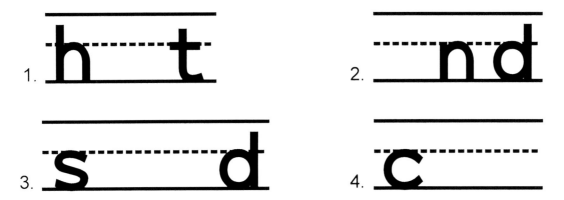

1. h _ t

2. _ n d

3. s _ d

4. c _

C. Write the list word shown in the picture.

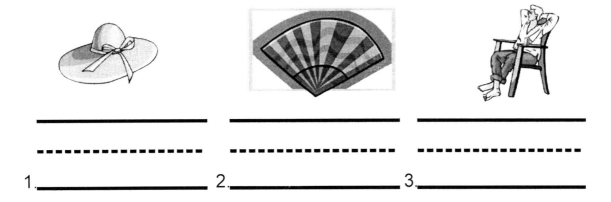

1. _____   2. _____   3. _____

Lesson 1
Day 3

sat	and	can
hat	sand	fan

A. Look at each picture. Write the list word that matches the beginning sound of the picture.

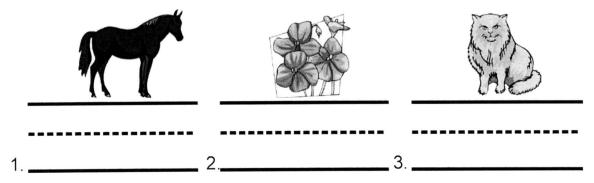

1. _____ 2. _____ 3. _____

B. Write the list word that rhymes with each given list word below.

1. sand   2. hat   3. can

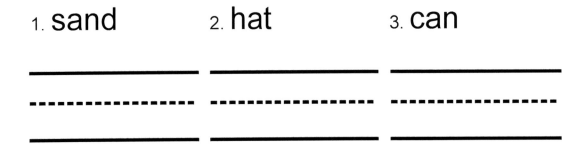

C. Copy the following sentence. **The fan blew the hat.**

Lesson 1
Day 4

sat	and	can
hat	sand	fan

A. Find and circle each list word in the puzzle below.

j	e	o	i	x	a
v	a	n	d	n	s
s	n	t	n	a	f
p	a	s	a	g	d
n	c	a	s	a	o
h	a	t	b	n	s

B. Unscramble and write the list words.

1. dsan

2. nda

3. tas

C. Copy the following sentence. **He put his hat in the can.**

Date: _____

• Final Test Lesson 1

Test: Correction Area:

1.

2.

3.

4.

5.

6.

**Lesson 2
Day 1**

Words with short vowel **e** sound

1. **Review Your List Words**
   Look at the list words below and read each word to yourself. Then review each definition.

List Words	Definitions
pen	• A device that writes with ink.
ten	• One more than nine.
end	• To conclude something or bring it to a close.
send	• To transmit something.
red	• A color in the rainbow.
bed	• Something you sleep on.

2. **Take Your Pretest**
   Turn to the next page to the Pretest section and your teacher will ask you to write each list word one at a time.

Pretest - Lesson 2:   Correction Area:

1.

2.

3.

4.

5.

6.

Carry-over Words: Correction Area:

7.

8.

Lesson 2
Day 2

pen	end	red
ten	send	bed

A. Find the list word in each string of letters.

npensa

1._____

tsendho

2._____

dbeder

3._____

rende

4._____

tredif

5._____

ftenhg

6._____

B. Write the following list words in alphabetical order.

red, ten, end

1._____ 2._____ 3._____

C. Complete the following list words. Use each list word only once.

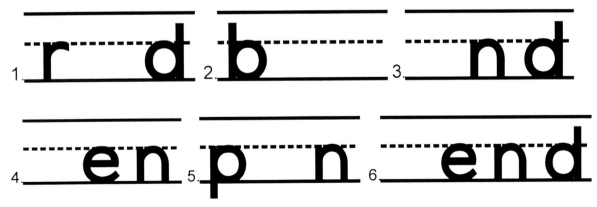

1. r__d   2. b____   3. ____nd

4. ____en   5. p__n   6. end

**Lesson 2
Day 3**

pen	end	red
ten	send	bed

A. Put the following list words in alphabetical order.

pen, bed, send

1._____ 2._____ 3._____

B. Write the list word that rhymes with each given list word.

send   **bed**   **pen**

1._____ 2._____ 3._____

C. Copy the following sentence. **The end of the pen was red.**

_____

_____

_____

_____

**Lesson 2
Day 4**

pen	end	red
ten	send	bed

A. Find and circle each list word in the puzzle below.

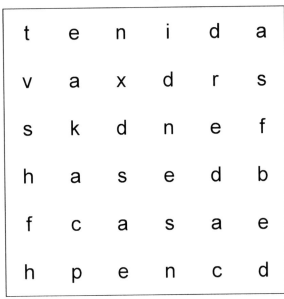

t	e	n	i	d	a
v	a	x	d	r	s
s	k	d	n	e	f
h	a	s	e	d	b
f	c	a	s	a	e
h	p	e	n	c	d

B. Find the list word in each string of letters.

asendc   nbeda   tpena

_____   _____   _____

- - - - - - - - -   - - - - - - - - -   - - - - - - - - -

1._____ 2._____ 3._____

C. Copy the following sentence. **She had to send ten boys to bed.**

_____

- -

_____

_____

- -

_____

_____

- -

_____

Lesson 2
Day 5

• Final Test Lesson 2

Correction Area:

1. _____

2. _____

3. _____

4. _____

5. _____

6. _____

Carry-over Words   Correction Area

7. _____

8. _____

Level 1, Lesson 2 – Words with short vowel **e** sound   12

**Lesson 3
Day 1**

Words with short vowel **i** sound

1. **Review Your List Words**
   Look at the list words below and read each word to yourself. Then review each definition.

List Words

pig

big

lip

tip

inn

ill

Definitions

- A swine animal.

- Large.

- The part of a face that surrounds the mouth. The rim or edge of something.

- A small portion of something. A small extra payment for good service.

- Temporary lodging. Similar to a hotel or motel room.

- Sick or not feeling well.

2. **Take Your Pretest**
   Turn to the next page to the Pretest section and your teacher will ask you to write each list word one at a time.

Pretest - Lesson 3:

Correction Area:

1.

2.

3.

4.

5.

6.

Carry-over Words:

Correction Area:

7.

8.

Lesson 3
Day 2

| pig | lip | inn |
| big | tip | ill |

A. Complete the following list words.

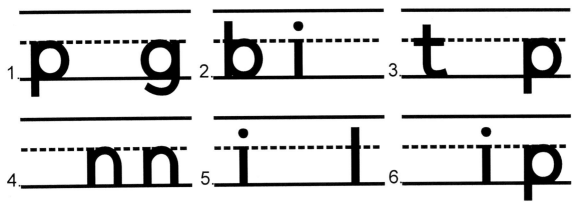

1. p   g   2. b i   3. t   p

4.   n n   5. i   6.   i p

B. Read the following sentence and write the list words you see.

The pig tail has a big curly tip.

1._____   2._____   3._____

C. Write the definition from Day 1 for the list word **ill**.

Lesson 3
Day 3

pig	lip	inn
big	tip	ill

A. Write the list word missing from these sentences.

_____

- -

1. The pig was _____ and heavy.

_____

- - - - - - - - - - - - - - - - - - - -

2. The _____ was a nice place to stay.

B. Underline the list word in each set of words that comes first in the alphabet. Write the underlined list words.

inn, big, lip   pig, tip, ill

_____   _____

- - - - - - - - - - - - - - -   - - - - - - - - - - - - - - - -

1._____   2._____

C. Copy the following sentence. **A tip was left for the inn.**

_____

- -

_____

_____

- -

_____

_____

- -

_____

Lesson 3
Day 4

| pig | lip | inn |
| big | tip | ill |

A. Look at each picture. Write the list word that matches the beginning sound
   of the picture.

1._____ 2._____ 3._____

B. Write the list word that matches each definition.

   A small portion of something.   Temporary lodging.

1. _____   2. _____

C. Copy the following sentence. **The ill pig had a big lip.**

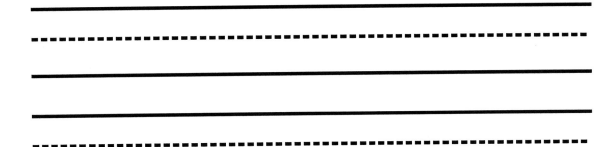

**Lesson 3
Day 5**

• Final Test Lesson 3

Correction Area:

1. _____

2. _____

3. _____

4. _____

5. _____

6. _____

Carry-over Words   Correction Area

7. _____

8. _____

Words with short vowel **o** sound

1. Review Your List Words

Look at the list words below and read each word to yourself. Then review each definition.

List Words	Definitions

List Words

pop

top

box

fox

hot

pot

Definitions

- A sharp quick noise. A type of drink.

- The highest point or position.

- A container that usually has four sides, a bottom, and a top.

- A small animal with pointy ears and a bushy tail.

- Having a high temperature.

- A container for cooking.

2. Take Your Pretest

Turn to the next page to the Pretest section and your teacher will ask you to write each list word one at a time.

Pretest - Lesson 4:   Correction Area:

1.

2.

3.

4.

5.

6.

Carry-over Words: Correction Area:

7.

8.

pop	box	pot
top	fox	hot

A. Underline the list words in the following sentences that are spelled incorrectly.

1. The door made a popp when closed.

2. The foxx was in the pond.

3. The toph of the can was open.

4. The potte was on the floor.

5. The hott sun was also bright.

6. The bxo had a toy in it.

B. Correctly write the above list words that are misspelled.

1. _____ 2. _____ 3. _____

4. _____ 5. _____ 6. _____

C. Unscramble the list words.

xfo   otp   ppo

1. _____ 2. _____ 3. _____

Lesson 4
Day 3

pop	box	pot
top	fox	hot

A. Write the list word that matches each definition.

A container for cooking.

The highest point.

Small animal with pointy ears.

1._____ 2._____ 3._____

B. Write the list word that rhymes with the given list word.

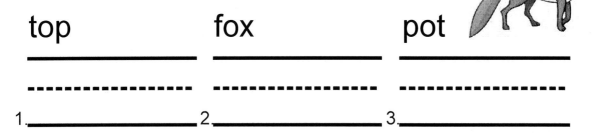

top   fox   pot

1._____ 2._____ 3._____

C. Copy the following sentence. **The top of the pot is hot.**

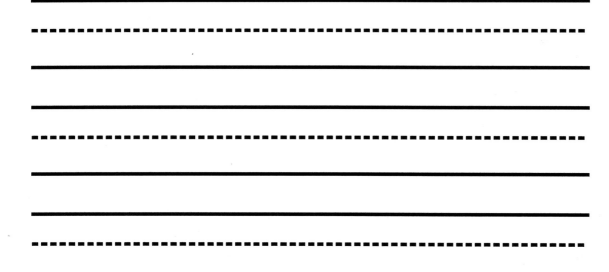

**Lesson 5
Day 1**

Words with short vowel **u** sound

1. **Review Your List Words**
   Look at the list words below and read each word to yourself. Then review each definition.

List Words

tug

rug

fun

run

bus

us

Definitions

- To pull on something.

- A floor covering.

- To do something enjoyable.

- To move fast on foot.

- A vehicle that carries many passengers.
- More than one person.

2. **Take Your Pretest**
   Turn to the next page to the Pretest section and your teacher will ask you to write each list word one at a time.

Pretest - Lesson 5:

Correction Area:

1.

2.

3.

4.

5.

6.

Carry-over Words:

Correction Area:

7.

8.

Lesson 5
Day 2

tug	fun	bus
rug	run	us

A. Write the two list words that end with the letter **n**.

1._____   2._____

B. Write the list words that name these pictures.

1. _____   2. _____

C. Write two list words that rhyme. (There is more than one pair.)

_____   _____

D. Write the definition from Day 1 for the list word **rug**.

_____

_____

Date: _____

Lesson 5
Day 3

tug	fun	bus
rug	run	us

A. Write the list word that is missing from these sentences.

_____

- - - - - - - - - - - - - - - - - -

1. The _____ is pretty on the floor.

_____

- - - - - - - - - - - - - - - - - -

2. The _____ carried many people.

B. Underline the list words in each sentence.

1. The dog chased us to the bus.

2. It is fun to run on the rug.

3. We will tug on the rope for fun.

C. Copy the following sentence. **It was fun to tug the rug.**

_____

- -

_____

- -

_____

**Lesson 5
Day 4**

tug	fun	bus
rug	run	us

A. Write two list words that start with a letter in the **A-L** alphabet range.

_____   _____

- - - - - - - - - - - - - - - -   - - - - - - - - - - - - - - - -

_____   _____

B. Write three list words that start with a letter in the **M-Z** alphabet range.

_____   _____   _____

- - - - - - - -   - - - - - - - -   - - - - - - - -

_____   _____   _____

C. Find and circle each list word in the puzzle below.

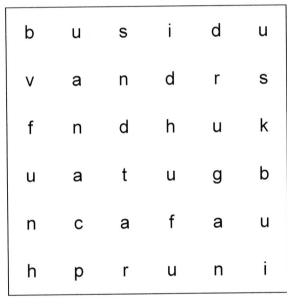

b	u	s	i	d	u
v	a	n	d	r	s
f	n	d	h	u	k
u	a	t	u	g	b
n	c	a	f	a	u
h	p	r	u	n	i

D. Copy the following sentence. **He will run us to the bus.**

_____

- -

_____

- -

_____

Lesson 5
Day 5

Final Test Lesson 5

Correction Area:

1. _____

2. _____

3. _____

4. _____

5. _____

6. _____

Carry-over Words   Correction Area

7. _____

8. _____

Lesson 6 Review Day 1

Review of words with short vowel **a** sound

List Words

sat	hat	and	sand	can	fan

A. Read the following sentence and write the list words you see.

He sat with his hat by the fan.

1. _____ 2. _____ 3. _____

B. Unscramble and write the list words.

1. dsan _____

2. nda _____

3. nac _____

C. Complete the list words.

1.  c ___ n

2.  c ___ t

3.  a ___ d

4.  s a n

Review of words with short vowel **e** sound

List Words

pen	ten	end	send	red	bed

A. Write a list word that has the same beginning sound as the picture.

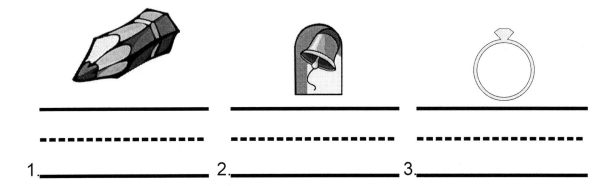

1._____ 2._____ 3._____

B. Write the list word that matches the definition.

1. A color in the rainbow.

_____

2. Something you sleep on.

_____

3. To transmit something.

_____

4. It writes with ink.

_____

5. A number one more than nine.

_____

6. To conclude something.

_____

Lesson 6
Review
Day 3

Review of words with short vowel **i** sound

List Words

pig	big	lip	tip	inn	ill

A. Underline the list words spelled incorrectly and write them correctly below.

1. The hat had a circular liip.

_____

- - - - - - - - - - - - - - - - -

_____

2. The pige was playful.

_____

- - - - - - - - - - - - - - - - -

_____

3. The inne had a room for us.

_____

- - - - - - - - - - - - - - - - -

_____

4. The bigg lion paced in the cage.

_____

- - - - - - - - - - - - - - - - -

_____

5. The child was il.

_____

- - - - - - - - - - - - - - - - -

_____

6. The tiph of the needle was sharp.

_____

- - - - - - - - - - - - - - - - -

_____

B. Write the word that does not rhyme.

1. **big, pig, tip**

_____

- - - - - - - - - - - -

_____

2. **lip, big, tip**

_____

- - - - - - - - - - - -

_____

Lesson 6
Review
Day 4

Review of words with short vowel **o** sound

List Words

| pop | top | box | fox | hot | pot |

A. Finish these words. Use each word only once.

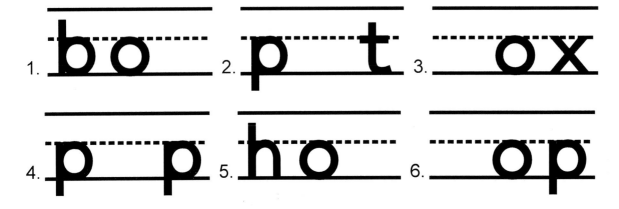

1. bo
2. p t
3. ox
4. p p
5. ho
6. op

B. Write the list word that belongs in each group.

1. dog, cat, wolf   2. bottom, side, front 3. cold, warm, cool

_____   _____   _____

- -

_____   _____   _____

C. Unscramble the list words.

xob   opt   opp

_____   _____   _____

- -

1._____ 2._____ 3._____

Lesson 6
Review
Day 5

Review of words with short vowel **u** sound

List Words

| tug | rug | fun | run | bus | us |

A. Write the list word that means the opposite of the word.

_____   _____

1. push _____   2. walk _____

_____   _____

3. boring _____   4. them _____

B. Write a list word to complete each sentence.

_____

1. She took the _____ to school.

_____

2. He spilled water on the _____ .

_____

3. We like to _____ and play.

_____

4. She spoke to _____ about the story.

Lesson 7 Day 1

Words with long vowel **a** sound

1. Review Your List Words

Look at the list words below and read each word to yourself. Then review each definition.

Notice that the vowel **e** is silent.

List Words	Definitions
take	• To get something back.
cake	• An iced treat made from baked dough.
cave	• An open horizontal space within the earth.
pave	• To layer a surface with a solid, rock-based covering.
place	• A space set aside for something.
trace	• A slight bit of something. To copy a picture by following its lines.

2. Take Your Pretest

Turn to the next page to the Pretest section and your teacher will ask you to write each list word one at a time.

Date: _____

Pretest - Lesson 7:

Correction Area:

1.

2.

3.

4.

5.

6.

Carry-over Words:

Correction Area:

7.

8.

Level 1, Lesson 7 – Words with long vowel **a** sound

38

Lesson 7
Day 2

take	cave	place
cake	pave	trace

A. Write the list words by adding and subtracting the letters. (Replace the letter from the same place where it was subtracted.)

Example: bake -b +t = take

make -m +c   gave -g +p   grace -g +t

_____   _____   _____

- - - - - - - - - - - - - -   - - - - - - - - - - - - - -   - - - - - - - - - - - - - -

1._____ 2._____ 3._____

B. Write the following list words in alphabetical order.

cave, take, place

_____   _____   _____

- - - - - - - - - - - - - -   - - - - - - - - - - - - - -   - - - - - - - - - - - - - -

1._____ 2._____ 3._____

C. Which picture below shows something you can eat? Write the list word below.

_____

- -

_____

Lesson 7
Day 3

| take | cave | place |
| cake | pave | trace |

A. Match the list words that begin with the same letter. Draw a line to connect each pair.

take   **cave**

cake   **place**

pave   **trace**

B. Copy the following sentence. **He will take the cake to his place.**

_____

- -

_____

- -

_____

- -

_____

C. Unscramble and write the list words.

1. apve   2. acetr   3. acve

_____   _____   _____

- - - - - - -   - - - - - - -   - - - - - - -

_____   _____   _____

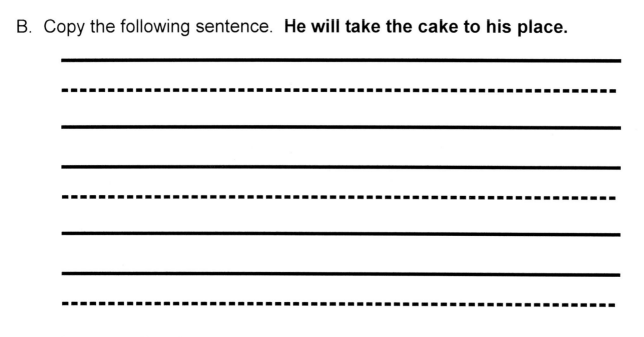

Lesson 7
Day 4

take   cave   place
cake   pave   trace

A. Write the two list words that start with a letter in the **A-L** alphabet range.

1._____   2._____

B. Write the four list words that start with a letter in the **M-Z** alphabet range.

1._____   2._____

3._____   4._____

C. Complete the list words.

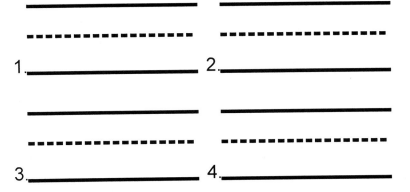

1. t__ac   2. c__ve

3. pl__e   4. t__k

D. Write the word that tells how to copy a picture.

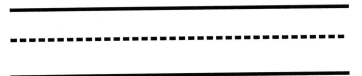

Date: _____

| • Final Test Lesson 7 |

Correction Area:

1. _____

2. _____

3. _____

4. _____

5. _____

6. _____

Carry-over Words   Correction Area

7. _____

8. _____

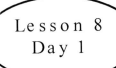

Lesson 8 Day 1

Words with long vowel **a** sound using **ay**

1. **Review Your List Words**
   Look at the list words below and read each word to yourself. Then review each definition.

List Words	**Definitions**
lay	• To set something down.
stay	• To remain in the same place.
play	• To have fun during an activity.
clay	• An earthy, sticky, moldable material.
away	• At a distance from another.
bay	• A part of a larger body of water that extends into land.

2. **Take Your Pretest**
   Turn to the next page to the Pretest section and your teacher will ask you to write each list word one at a time.

Date: _____

Pretest - Lesson 8:

Correction Area:

1.

2.

3.

4.

5.

6.

Carry-over Words:

Correction Area:

7.

8.

Lesson 8
Day 2

lay	play	away
stay	clay	bay

A. Complete the following sentences with list words.

_____

- - - - - - - - - - - -

1. Will you _____ my coat on the couch?

_____

- - - - - - - - - - - - - - -

2. The children like to run and _____ with the puppy.

_____

- - - - - - - - - - - -

3. We sailed through the _____ with our boat.

_____

- - - - - - - - - - - - - -

4. We ran _____ from the rushing water.

B. Copy the following sentence. **They wanted to stay and play with clay.**

_____

- -

_____

_____

- -

_____

_____

- -

_____

Level 1, Lesson 8 – Words with long vowel **a** sound using **ay**

**Lesson 8
Day 3**

lay	play	away
stay	clay	bay

A. Find and circle each list word in the puzzle below.

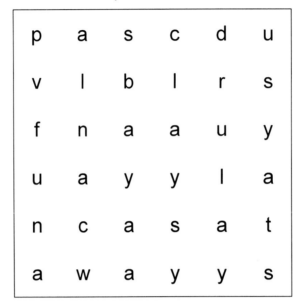

p	a	s	c	d	u
v	l	b	l	r	s
f	n	a	a	u	y
u	a	y	y	l	a
n	c	a	s	a	t
a	w	a	y	y	s

B. Read the following sentence and write the list words you see.

The children put the clay away after they play.

1._____ 2._____ 3._____

C. Write the list words in alphabetical order.

1._____ 2._____ 3._____

4._____ 5._____ 6._____

**Lesson 8
Day 4**

lay	play	away
stay	clay	bay

A. Complete the list words.

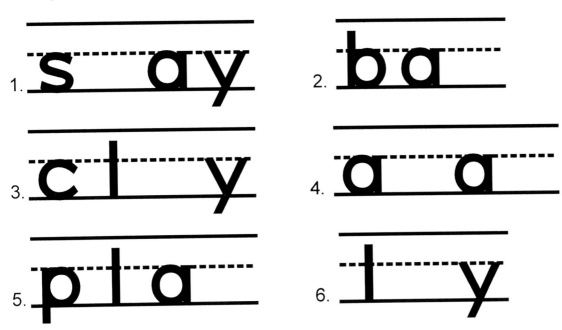

1. s ay

2. ba

3. cly

4. a a

5. pta

6. ty

B. Copy the following sentence. **The clay beach on the bay was nice.**

Lesson 8
Day 5

| Final Test Lesson 9 |

Correction Area:

1. _____

2. _____

3. _____

4. _____

5. _____

6. _____

Carry-over Words   Correction Area

7. _____

8. _____

Lesson 9
Day 1

Words with long vowel **a** sound using **ai**

1. **Review Your List Words**
Look at the list words below and read each word to yourself. Then review each definition.

When **a** and another vowel are side by side, the **a** vowel usually makes its long sound and the second vowel is usually silent.

List Words

| paid |
| maid |
| pain |
| wait |
| fair |
| mail |

Definitions

- To have given an amount of money for something.
- One who cleans for payment.

- A feeling of hurt or discomfort.

- To stay in one place until something happens.
- A fun place with amusement rides and entertaining attractions.
- Letters, parcels, or paper sent from one person to another.

2. **Take Your Pretest**
Turn to the next page to the Pretest section and your teacher will ask you to write each list word one at a time.

Date: _____

Pretest - Lesson 9:   Correction Area:

1.

2.

3.

4.

5.

6.

Carry-over Words: Correction Area:

7.

8.

paid	pain	fair
maid	wait	mail

A. Match each list word with its definition. Draw a line to connect each pair.

paid   One who cleans for payment.

wait   A feeling of hurt or discomfort.

maid   To have given an amount of money for something.

mail   To stay in one place until something happens.

pain   A fun place with amusement rides and entertaining attractions.

fair   Letters, parcel, or paper sent from one person to another.

B. Take the short vowel out and replace it with **ai**. Write the list word.

Example: pen –e +ai = paid

1. wet

2. mil

3. mad

4. fur

5. pad

6. pan

Date: _____

Lesson 9
Day 3

paid	pain	fair
maid	wait	mail

A. Complete the following sentence with list words. Use each word only once.

_____

- -

1. The _____ cleaned the room at the inn.

_____

- -

2. Ted got a card from Jill in the _____.

_____

- -

3. He sat on the curb to _____ for the parade.

_____

- - - - - - - - - - - - - - - - - -

4. We _____ for the food and drink with cash.

_____

- - - - - - - - - - - - - - - - - -

5. The girl was in _____ after falling off the step.

B. Read the following sentences and write the list words you see.

She paid for a ticket to the fair. She had to wait to go.

_____ _____ _____

- - - - - - - - - - -   - - - - - - - - - - -   - - - - - - - - - - -

1._____ 2._____ 3._____

Lesson 9
Day 4

paid	pain	fair
maid	wait	mail

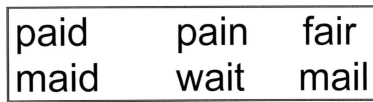

A. Complete the list words. Use each list word only once.

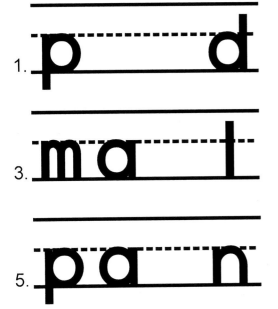

1. p _ _ d

2. w _ _ t

3. m a _ l

4. m _ _ d

5. p a _ n

6. f _ _ r

B. Copy the following sentence. **The maid was paid for her work at the inn.**

Date: _____

• Final Test Lesson 9

Correction Area:

1. _____

2. _____

3. _____

4. _____

5. _____

6. _____

Carry-over Words   Correction Area

7. _____

8. _____

Lesson 10
Day 1

Words with long vowel **u** sound

1. Review Your List Words
Look at the list words below and read each word to yourself. Then review each definition.

Notice that the vowel **e** is silent.

List Words	Definitions
rule	• A law or rigid guideline.
mule	• Offspring of a donkey and horse.
tube	• A soft squeezable container which holds something inside.
cube	• A solid body having six equal sides.
cure	• Recovery from a disease.
sure	• Confident, having no doubt.

2. Take Your Pretest
Turn to the next page to the Pretest section and your teacher will ask you to write each list word one at a time.

Pretest - Lesson 10:

Correction Area:

1.

2.

3.

4.

5.

6.

Carry-over Words:

Correction Area:

7.

8.

**Lesson 10
Day 2**

rule	tube	cure
mule	cube	sure

A. Write three sets of list words that rhyme with each other.

1. __cure__ _____

2. _____ _____

3. _____ __cube__

B. Write the list word from each group of similar words.

1. horse, mule, donkey   2. box, square, cube   3. rule, law, command

_____   _____   _____

C. Read the following sentence and write the list words you see.

He could cure the mule with a tube of medicine.

1. _____   2. _____   3. _____

Lesson 10
Day 3

rule	tube	cure
mule	cube	sure

A. Complete the following sentences with list words.

1. The _____ was hard to roll since it was square.

2. He was _____ he knew the answer.

3. The _____ of toothpaste was on the shelf.

4. There was a _____ that said no running in the house.

B. Copy the following sentence. **He used a tube of cream to cure the mule.**

Lesson 10
Day 4

rule	tube	cure
mule	cube	sure

A. Complete the list words. Use each list word only once.

1. r u _ _ _

2. t _ _ e

3. m _ l e

4. c _ _ r e

5. s _ _ r e

6. c _ _ e

B. Copy the following sentence. **I was sure I knew the rule for the game cube.**

Level 1, Lesson 10 – Words with long vowel **u** sound

59

• Final Test Lesson 10

Correction Area:

1. _____

2. _____

3. _____

4. _____

5. _____

6. _____

Carry-over Words   Correction Area

7. _____

8. _____

**Lesson 11
Day 1**

Words with long vowel **u**
sound using **ew**

1. **Review Your List Words**
   Look at the list words below and read each word to yourself. Then review each definition.

List Words	Definitions
new	• Not used before.
knew	• Had knowledge.
few	• Not many, but some. More than two of something.
flew	• To have flown in the air.
dew	• Moisture that sticks to objects during the night, such as plants.
drew	• To have drawn something, like a picture. Past tense of draw.

2. **Take Your Pretest**
   Turn to the next page to the Pretest section and your teacher will ask you to write each list word one at a time.

Pretest - Lesson 11:

Correction Area:

1.

2.

3.

4.

5.

6.

Carry-over Words:

Correction Area:

7.

8.

Lesson 11
Day 2

new	few	dew
knew	flew	drew

A. Find the words that look similar. Notice how even though they look similar, they have very different meanings. Draw a line to connect each pair.

new   flew

drew   knew

few   dew

B. Underline the list word that is spelled incorrectly and write it correctly below. (Make sure the meaning of the list word is correct. See the definitions.)

1. He kneww the answer.

    _____

    -

    _____

2. The toy was newe.

    _____

    -

    _____

3. The leaf had deww on it.

    _____

    -

    _____

4. She dreuw a picture of the dog.

    _____

    -

    _____

5. The bird flewe in the blue sky.

    _____

    -

    _____

6. He had a feuw toys in the box.

    _____

    -

    _____

| new | few | dew |
| knew | flew | drew |

A. Unscramble the list words. Write the correct list words below.

lfwe

1._____

derw

2._____

newk

3._____

wde

4._____

nwe

5._____

wef

6._____

B. Underline the list words in this sentence that are misspelled or used incorrectly.

The bird new as it flewe that it was looking for a feww worms in the deww.

C. Copy the following sentence. **A few of the new toys flew.**

_____

_____

_____

_____

_____

_____

**Lesson 11
Day 4**

new	few	dew
knew	flew	drew

A. Write the list word that matches each definition.

1. Not used before.

   _____

2. Had knowledge.

   _____

3. To have drawn something.

   _____

4. To have flown in the air.

   _____

5. Moisture on plants.

   _____

6. Not many, but some.

   _____

B. Copy the following sentence. **He knew that she drew a picture.**

_____

_____

_____

Level 1, Lesson 11 – Words with long vowel **u** sound using **ew**

Date: _____

• Final Test Lesson 11

Correction Area:

1. _____

2. _____

3. _____

4. _____

5. _____

6. _____

Carry-over Words   Correction Area

7. _____

8. _____

Lesson 12 Review Day 1

Review of words with long vowel **a** sound

List Words

| take | cake | cave | pave | place | trace |

A. Unscramble and write the list words.

1. etka

_____

- - - - - - - - - - - - - - - - -

_____

2. pclea

_____

- - - - - - - - - - - - - - - - -

_____

3. trcea

_____

- - - - - - - - - - - - - - - - -

_____

4. vcea

_____

- - - - - - - - - - - - - - - - -

_____

B. Write two list words that rhyme with each word below.

_____   _____
- - - - - - - - - - - -   - - - - - - - - - - - -

1. gave _____   _____

_____   _____
- - - - - - - - - - - -   - - - - - - - - - - - -

2. face _____   _____

_____   _____
- - - - - - - - - - - -   - - - - - - - - - - - -

3. rake _____   _____

Lesson 12
Review
Day 2

Review of words with long vowel **a** sound using **ay**

List Words

| lay | stay | play | clay | away | bay |

A. Finish these words.

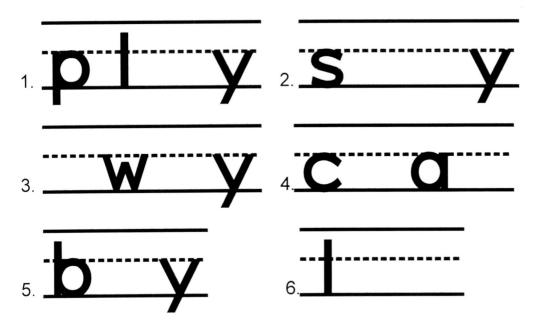

1. p l ___ y
2. s ___ ___ y
3. ___ w ___ y
4. c ___ a ___
5. b ___ y
6. ___ ___ t ___

B. Unscramble and write the list words.

lcya

1. _____

yba

2. _____

aawy

3. _____

lpya

4. _____

lya

5. _____

tsay

6. _____

Lesson 12 Review Day 3

Review of words with long vowel **a** sound using **ai**

List Words

paid	maid	pain	wait	fair	mail

A. Write one list word that rhymes.

1. **bait, gait**

   _____

   - - - - - - - - - - - - - - - - - -

   _____

2. **rain, gain**

   _____

   - - - - - - - - - - - - - - - - - -

   _____

3. **hair, pair**

   _____

   - - - - - - - - - - - - - - - - - -

   _____

4. **nail, sail**

   _____

   - - - - - - - - - - - - - - - - - -

   _____

B. Underline the list word that is spelled incorrectly and write it correctly below.

1. He was pade for his work.

   _____

   -

   _____

2. The maide cleaned the room.

   _____

   -

   _____

3. She had to waiht for the bus.

   _____

   -

   _____

4. The maail arrived early.

   _____

   -

   _____

5. They had fun at the faire.

   _____

   -

   _____

6. She was in some paine.

   _____

   -

   _____

Lesson 12
Review
Day 4

Review of words with long vowel
u sound

List Words

| rule | mule | tube | cube | cure | sure |

A. Write a list word that has the same beginning sound as the picture.

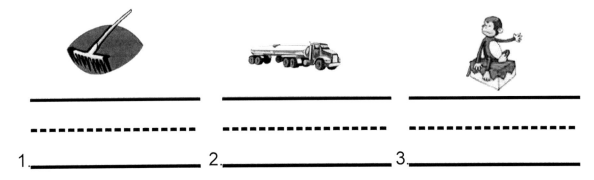

1._____ 2._____ 3._____

B. Write the word that matches each definition.

1. A law or rigid guideline.

_____

_____

2. A squeezable container.

_____

_____

3. Offspring of a donkey and horse.

_____

_____

4. A solid body having six
   equal sides.

_____

_____

5. Recovery from a disease.

_____

_____

6. Confident, having no doubt.

_____

_____

Lesson 12
Review
Day 5

Review of words with long vowel **u** sound using **ew**

List Words

| new | knew | few | flew | dew | drew |

A. Complete the following sentences with the correct list word. Use each list word only once.

1. The bird _____ across the sky.

2. The toy was _____ for his birthday.

3. She _____ the answer to the test question.

4. The leaf had _____ on it during the night.

5. We had a _____ questions for the teacher.

6. The artist _____ a picture of the girl.

<<Intentionally left blank>>

Words with long vowel **e** sound

1. **Review Your List Words**
   Look at the list words below and read each word to yourself. Then review each definition.

List Words

redo
she
we
me
be
he

Definitions

- To try again. Do over.

- Refers to a female (girl) person or animal.

- Refers to a group of people. Similar to the word us.

- Used when referring to yourself.

- To live or exist.

- Refers to a male (boy) person or animal.

2. **Take Your Pretest**
   Turn to the next page to the Pretest section and your teacher will ask you to write each list word one at a time.

Pretest - Lesson 13:

Correction Area:

1.

2.

3.

4.

5.

6.

Carry-over Words:

Correction Area:

7.

8.

Lesson 13
Day 2

redo	we	be
she	me	he

A. Take the out the long vowel sound and replace it with **e**. Write the list word. The first one has been done for you.

Example: hi -i +e = he

1. my   2. by   3. shy

B. Read the following sentences and write the list words you see.

He and she saw me at the fair.

1._____ 2._____ 3._____

C. Copy the following sentence. **We had to redo our art project.**

**Lesson 13
Day 3**

redo	we	be
she	me	he

A. Complete the sentences with list words.

1. _____ cleaned her room. (refers to a girl)

2. Dad took Ted and _____ to the zoo. (refers to yourself)

3. _____ sat in his chair. (refers to a boy)

4. We had to _____ our work since it was incorrect.

5. He wanted to _____ next to his dad.

B. Write a list word that has the same beginning sound as the picture.

1._____ 2._____ 3._____

Lesson 13
Day 4

redo	we	be
she	me	he

A. Write the list word that matches each definition.

1. Refers to a girl.

_____

- - - - - - - - - - - - - - - - -

_____

2. Referring to yourself.

_____

- - - - - - - - - - - - - - - - -

_____

3. Similar to the word us.

_____

- - - - - - - - - - - - - - - - -

_____

4. To live or exist.

_____

- - - - - - - - - - - - - - - - -

_____

5. To try again. Do over.

_____

- - - - - - - - - - - - - - - - -

_____

6. Refers to a boy.

_____

- - - - - - - - - - - - - - - - -

_____

B. Copy the following sentence. **He said she would be by me.**

_____

- -

_____

- -

_____

- -

_____

Lesson 13
Day 5

• Final Test Lesson 13

Correction Area:

1. _____

2. _____

3. _____

4. _____

5. _____

6. _____

Carry-over Words   Correction Area

7. _____

8. _____

Level 1, Lesson 13 – Words with long vowel **e** sound

**Lesson 14
Day 1**

Words with long vowel **e** sound using **ee**

1. **Review Your List Words**
   Look at the list words below and read each word to yourself. Then review each definition.

List Words	Definitions
seed	• A source of plant growth.
need	• Something that must be done.
feel	• To touch something.
heel	• The back part of a human foot.
see	• To have visual sight.
bee	• A striped insect that stings.

2. **Take Your Pretest**
   Turn to the next page to the Pretest section and your teacher will ask you to write each list word one at a time.

Pretest - Lesson 14:

Correction Area:

1.

2.

3.

4.

5.

6.

Carry-over Words:

Correction Area:

7.

8.

Lesson 14
Day 2

seed	feel	see
need	heel	bee

A. Read the following sentences and underline the words with the **ee** sound. Write the list words you find.

I see that I need to seed the garden.

1. _____ 2. _____ 3. _____

Joe could feel the bee under his heel.

4. _____ 5. _____ 6. _____

B. Copy the following sentence. **We could see the bee near the seed.**

_____

_____

_____

_____

Lesson 14
Day 3

seed	feel	see
need	heel	bee

A. Write a list word that matches the definition.

   1. To have visual sight.

      _____

   2. The back part of a foot.

      _____

   3. A stinging insect.

      _____

   4. To touch something.

      _____

   5. Source of plant growth.

      _____

   6. Something that must be done.

      _____

B. Write a list word that has the same beginning sound as the picture.

1._____   2._____   3._____

Lesson 14
Day 4

seed	feel	see
need	heel	bee

A. Write a list word to finish each sentence.

_____

1. The farmer planted the _____ in his field.

_____

2. The _____ stung the boy on his hand.

_____

3. She could _____ the warm sun on her face.

_____

4. His _____ was sore from running.

B. Copy the following sentence. **He could see the need for more seed.**

_____

_____

_____

_____

**Lesson 14
Day 5**

• Final Test Lesson 14

Correction Area:

1. _____

2. _____

3. _____

4. _____

5. _____

6. _____

Carry-over Words   Correction Area

7. _____

8. _____

Lesson 15
Day 1

| Words with long vowel **i** sound |

1. Review Your List Words

Look at the list words below and read each word to yourself. Then review each definition.

Notice that the vowel **e** is silent.

List Words   **Definitions**

five
hive
dime
time
bite
kite

- One more than four.

- A place where bees live.

- A coin worth ten cents.

- An hour, minute, or second as measured by a clock.

- To capture with teeth.

- A toy that flies in the air carried by wind.

2. Take Your Pretest

Turn to the next page to the Pretest section and your teacher will ask you to write each list word one at a time.

Date: _____

Pretest - Lesson 15:   Correction Area:

1. _____   _____

2. _____   _____

3. _____   _____

4. _____   _____

5. _____   _____

6. _____   _____

Carry-over Words: Correction Area:

7. _____   _____

8. _____   _____

Lesson 15
Day 2

five	dime	bite
hive	time	kite

A. Write the list word that matches each picture.

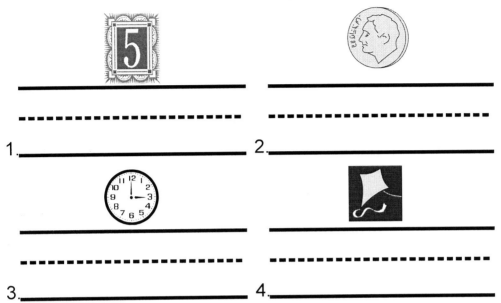

1._____   2._____

3._____   4._____

B.   Read the sentence and write the list words below:

The hungry bear took a bite out of the hive.

1._____   2._____

C. Write the definition from Day 1 for the list word **dime**.

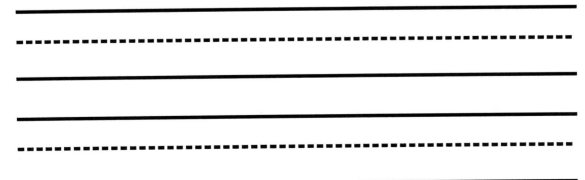

Level 1, Lesson 15 – Words with long vowel **i** sound

87

Lesson 15
Day 3

Date: _____

five	dime	bite
hive	time	kite

A. Write a list word that matches each definition.

1. One more than four.

_____

- - - - - - - - - - - - - - - - - -

_____

2. A coin worth ten cents.

_____

- - - - - - - - - - - - - - - - - -

_____

3. An hour, a minute,
   a second.

_____

- - - - - - - - - - - - - - - - - -

_____

4. A toy that flies in the air carried
   by the wind.

_____

- - - - - - - - - - - - - - - - - -

_____

5. To grab with teeth.

_____

- - - - - - - - - - - - - - - - - -

_____

6. Where bees live.

_____

- - - - - - - - - - - - - - - - - -

_____

B. Write a list word that has the same beginning sound as the picture.

1._____ 2._____ 3._____

Lesson 15
Day 4

five	dime	bite
hive	time	kite

A. Find and circle each list word in the puzzle below.

f	u	t	i	m	e
i	s	o	d	i	h
v	e	h	i	v	e
e	a	u	m	e	t
i	n	a	e	c	i
k	i	t	e	a	b

B. Unscramble and write the list words.

1. demi

2. fiev

3. ibte

C. Copy the following sentence. **This time he flew his kite by the hive.**

Lesson 15
Day 5

• Final Test Lesson 15

Correction Area:

1. _____

2. _____

3. _____

4. _____

5. _____

6. _____

Carry-over Words   Correction Area

7. _____

8. _____

**Lesson 16
Day 1**

Words with long vowel **o** sound

1. **Review Your List Words**

   Look at the list words below and read each word to yourself. Then review each definition.

   Notice that the vowel **e** is silent.

List Words	**Definitions**
rope	• Strands of cord twisted together.
hope	• A desire for something.
cone	• A circular shape that tapers to a point.
tone	• The quality of sound you hear.
poke	• To jab or thrust at something.
joke	• Saying or doing something funny.

2. **Take Your Pretest**

   Turn to the next page to the Pretest section and your teacher will ask you to write each list word one at a time.

Pretest - Lesson 16:   Correction Area:

1.

2.

3.

4.

5.

6.

Carry-over Words: Correction Area:

7.

8.

Lesson 16
Day 2

rope	cone	poke
hope	tone	joke

A. Find and circle each list word in the puzzle below.

r	o	p	e	t	c
t	e	o	n	o	o
e	n	k	n	n	e
o	j	e	h	e	k
p	k	t	j	k	o
h	o	p	e	h	j

B. Write the list words that rhyme with the words in bold. The first one is done for you.

1. **bone** ___cone___ _____

2. **nope** _____ _____

3. **spoke** _____ _____

Lesson 16
Day 3

rope	cone	poke
hope	tone	joke

A. Write a list word that matches each definition.

1. Strands of a cord twisted
   together.

   _____

   - - - - - - - - - - - - - - - -

   _____

2. Circular shape that tapers
   to a point.

   _____

   - - - - - - - - - - - - - - - -

   _____

3. The quality of sound.

   _____

   - - - - - - - - - - - - - - - -

   _____

4. Saying or doing something funny.

   _____

   - - - - - - - - - - - - - - - -

   _____

5. A desire for something.

   _____

   - - - - - - - - - - - - - - - -

   _____

6. To jab or thrust at something.

   _____

   - - - - - - - - - - - - - - - -

   _____

B. Copy the following sentence. **By the tone of his voice it was a joke.**

   _____

   -

   _____

   _____

   -

   _____

   _____

   -

   _____

Lesson 16
Day 4

| rope | cone | poke |
| hope | tone | joke |

A. Write the list words by adding and subtracting the letters.

nope -n +h

_____

- - - - - - - - - - - - - - - -

1._____

bone -b +c

_____

- - - - - - - - - - - - - - - -

2._____

jolt -lt +ke

_____

- - - - - - - - - - - - - - - -

3._____

joke -j +p

_____

- - - - - - - - - - - - - - - -

4._____

nope -n +r

_____

- - - - - - - - - - - - - - - -

5._____

take -ak +on

_____

- - - - - - - - - - - - - - - -

6._____

B. Write the definition from Day 1 for the list word **joke**.

_____

- -

_____

- -

_____

- -

_____

**Lesson 16
Day 5**

| • Final Test Lesson 16 |

Correction Area:

1. _____

2. _____

3. _____

4. _____

5. _____

6. _____

Carry-over Words

Correction Area

7. _____

8. _____

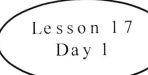

Lesson 17
Day 1

Words with long vowel **o** sound using **oa**

1. **Review Your List Words**
   Look at the list words below and read each word to yourself. Then review each definition.

List Words	Definitions

List Words

boat

coat

toad

load

coal

foal

Definitions

- A vessel that floats and moves across the water under power.

- An outer cover worn to stay warm.

- An amphibian that likes to hop and usually lives on land.

- Something that is picked up and carried.

- A black, solid mineral that is able to be burned.

- A young horse under a year old.

2. **Take Your Pretest**
   Turn to the next page to the Pretest section and your teacher will ask you to write each list word one at a time.

Pretest - Lesson 17:

Correction Area:

1. _____

2. _____

3. _____

4. _____

5. _____

6. _____

Carry-over Words:

Correction Area:

7. _____

8. _____

Lesson 17
Day 2

boat	toad	coal
coat	load	foal

A. Find and circle each list word in the puzzle below.

b	l	o	d	a	o
a	o	f	a	l	f
l	a	a	o	c	o
t	d	a	t	o	a
b	o	t	o	a	l
c	o	a	t	l	o

B. Find two list words above that rhyme with each word in bold.

goat

1. _____ 2. _____

road

3. _____ 4. _____

goal

5. _____ 6. _____

Lesson 17 Day 3

boat	toad	coal
coat	load	foal

A. Write a list word that matches each definition.

1. A vessel that floats.

2. A young horse.

3. Something that is picked up and carried.

4. Outer cover worn to stay warm.

5. An amphibian.

6. Black solid material that burns.

B. Copy the following sentence. **The boat carried a big load of coal.**

Lesson 17
Day 4

boat	toad	coal
coat	load	foal

A. Write list words by adding and subtracting the letters. Replace the new letters in the same place that they are subtracted.

goat -g +c   road -r +t   goal -g +c

1._____   2._____   3._____

look -ok +ad   moat -m +b   fall -al +oa

4._____   5._____   6._____

B. Write the definition from Day 1 for the list word **coat**.

_____

_____

_____

_____

_____

_____

Lesson 17
Day 5

• Final Test Lesson 17

Correction Area:

1. _____   _____

2. _____   _____

3. _____   _____

4. _____   _____

5. _____   _____

6. _____   _____

Carry-over Words   Correction Area

7. _____   _____

8. _____   _____

Lesson 18
Review
Day 1

Review of words with long vowel **e** sound

List Words

redo	she	we	me	be	he

A. Write the list word that does not rhyme with the others.

_____

- - - - - - - - - - - - - - - -

_____

B. Underline the list words spelled incorrectly and write them correctly below.

1. Tom had to redoe his work.

_____

- - - - - - - - - - - - - - - - -

_____

2. It would have to bea him.

_____

- - - - - - - - - - - - - - - - - - -

_____

3. Whee all had to wait.

_____

- - - - - - - - - - - - - - - - -

_____

4. Shie grew tall.

_____

- - - - - - - - - - - - - - - - -

_____

5. Heh had fun at the fair.

_____

- - - - - - - - - - - - - - - - - -

_____

6. Sally gave candy to mei.

_____

- - - - - - - - - - - - - - - - - -

_____

C. Write the following list words in alphabetical order.

redo, she, me

_____   _____   _____

- - - - - - - - - - - - -   - - - - - - - - - - - - -   - - - - - - - - - - - - -

1._____   2._____   3._____

Review of words with long vowel **e** sound using **ee**

List Words

seed	need	feel	heel	see	bee

A. Correct the sentences by underlining the word that does not make sense and replace it with a list word.

1. He could not fell his toes because they were cold. _____

2. She could not sea her hand because it was dark. _____

3. His hill hurt from running too much. _____

4. He planted the sed in the field to grow. _____

5. She would kneed a ride since her house was far. _____

6. The be stung her on the hand. _____

Lesson 18 Review Day 3

Review of words with long vowel i sound

List Words

| five | hive | dime | time | bite | kite |

A. Write the list word that rhymes with each given list word below.

five
_____
- - - - - - - - - - - - - - -
1. _____

bite
_____
- - - - - - - - - - - - - - -
2. _____

time
_____
- - - - - - - - - - - - - - -
3. _____

kite
_____
- - - - - - - - - - - - - - -
4. _____

dime
_____
- - - - - - - - - - - - - - -
5. _____

hive
_____
- - - - - - - - - - - - - - -
6. _____

B. Write a list word that matches each definition.

1. One more than four.
_____
- - - - - - - - - - - - - - -
_____

2. A coin worth ten cents.
_____
- - - - - - - - - - - - - - -
_____

3. To capture with teeth.
_____
- - - - - - - - - - - - - - -
_____

4. A place where bees live.
_____
- - - - - - - - - - - - - - -
_____

5. A toy that flies high in the sky.
_____
- - - - - - - - - - - - - - -
_____

6. A second, a minute, an hour.
_____
- - - - - - - - - - - - - - -
_____

Lesson 18
Review
Day 4

| Review of words with long vowel **o** sound |

List Words

| rope | hope | cone | tone | poke | joke |

A. Finish these words.

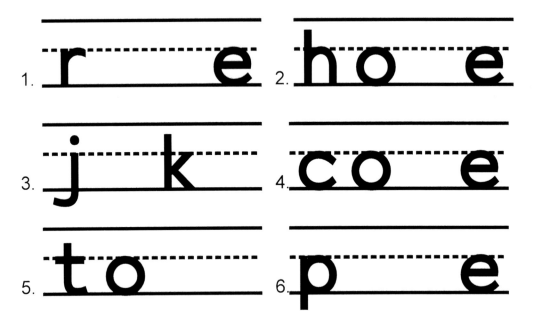

1. r ___ e ___

2. h o ___ e

3. j ___ k ___

4. c o ___ e

5. t o ___

6. p ___ e

B. Unscramble the list words.

orpe

1. _____

peko

2. _____

hpoe

3. _____

tneo

4. _____

ekoj

5. _____

eocn

6. _____

Lesson 18
Review
Day 5

Review of words with long vowel **o** sound using **oa**

List Words

| boat | coat | toad | load | coal | foal |

A. Write a list word to finish each sentence.

_____

- -

1. The farmer took a _____ of corn to the market.

_____

- - - - - - - - - - - - - - - - - - -

2. The _____ had warts all over its body.

_____

- -

3. The mother horse gave birth to a _____ .

_____

- -

4. The furnace needed more _____ to burn.

B. Write a list word that describes each picture.

_____   _____   _____

- - - - - - - - - -   - - - - - - - - - -   - - - - - - - - - -

1._____ 2._____ 3._____

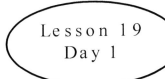

Lesson 19
Day 1

Words with long vowel **o** sound using **ow**

1. **Review Your List Words**
   Look at the list words below and read each word to yourself. Then review each definition.

List Words

Definitions

low	• Not high, short.
bow	• An arched weapon used for shooting arrows.
row	• To make a boat glide across the water by using one or more oars.
mow	• To cut the grass in a lawn.
bowl	• A dish with sides that holds food.
snow	• Frozen precipitation that falls to the ground.

2. **Take Your Pretest**
   Turn to the next page to the Pretest section and your teacher will ask you to write each list word one at a time.

Pretest - Lesson 19:   Correction Area:

1.

2.

3.

4.

5.

6.

Carry-over Words: Correction Area:

7.

8.

Lesson 19
Day 2

| low | row | bowl |
| bow | mow | snow |

A. Find the list word in each string of letters. Write the list words below.

allowed   arrow   mowing

‒‒‒‒‒‒‒‒‒‒‒‒‒‒   ‒‒‒‒‒‒‒‒‒‒‒‒‒‒   ‒‒‒‒‒‒‒‒‒‒‒‒‒‒

- - - - - - - - - - - -   - - - - - - - - - - - -   - - - - - - - - - - - -

1._____ 2._____ 3._____

B. Write the list word shown in the picture.

‒‒‒‒‒‒‒‒‒‒‒‒‒‒   ‒‒‒‒‒‒‒‒‒‒‒‒‒‒   ‒‒‒‒‒‒‒‒‒‒‒‒‒‒

- - - - - - - - - - - -   - - - - - - - - - - - -   - - - - - - - - - - - -

1._____ 2._____ 3._____

C. Find and circle each list word in the puzzle below.

e	a	n	r	m	s
b	n	e	m	o	d
o	s	n	o	w	r
w	i	l	e	b	o
l	g	o	b	o	w
a	u	w	o	s	i

Level 1, Lesson 19 – Words with long vowel **o** sound using **ow**

111

Lesson 19 Day 3

low	row	bowl
bow	mow	snow

A. Write a list word that matches each definition.

1. Frozen precipitation.

_____

- - - - - - - - - - - - - - -

_____

2. A weapon used to shoot arrows.

_____

- - - - - - - - - - - - - - -

_____

3. To cut the grass.

_____

- - - - - - - - - - - - - - -

_____

4. Not high, short.

_____

- - - - - - - - - - - - - - -

_____

5. To make a boat move with oars.

_____

- - - - - - - - - - - - - - -

_____

6. A dish with sides.

_____

- - - - - - - - - - - - - - -

_____

B. Copy the following sentence. **She tried to row her boat in the snow.**

_____

- -

_____

- -

_____

- -

_____

Lesson 19
Day 4

low	row	bowl
bow	mow	snow

A. Write the list words by adding and subtracting the letters.

know -k +s   cow -c +r   now -n +b

_____   _____   _____

- - - - - - - - - -   - - - - - - - - - -   - - - - - - - - - -

1._____   2._____   3._____

how -h +l   tow -t +m   fowl -f +b

_____   _____   _____

- - - - - - - - - -   - - - - - - - - - -   - - - - - - - - - -

4._____   5._____   6._____

B. Write the definition from Day 1 for the list word **snow**.

_____

- -

_____

_____

- -

_____

_____

- -

_____

Lesson 19
Day 5

• Final Test Lesson 19

Correction Area:

1.

2.

3.

4.

5.

6.

Carry-over Words

Correction Area

7.

8.

Level 1, Lesson 19 – Words with long vowel **o** sound using **ow**

114

Lesson 20
Day 1

Words with soft **g** sound

1. Review Your List Words
Look at the list words below and read each word to yourself. Then review each definition.

Notice that the **g** in these list words actually makes a **j** sound.

List Words	Definitions
gem	• A valuable, shiny stone for jewelry.
germ	• A very small microbe that can cause sickness in the body.
ginger	• A hot spice made from the root of a tropical plant.
gender	• Condition of being male or female.
giant	• Much larger than usual.
gym	• A room or building for sports.

2. Take Your Pretest
Turn to the next page to the Pretest section and your teacher will ask you to write each list word one at a time.

Pretest - Lesson 20:   Correction Area:

1.

2.

3.

4.

5.

6.

Carry-over Words: Correction Area:

7.

8.

Lesson 20
Day 2

gem	ginger	giant
germ	gender	gym

A. Find and circle each list word in the puzzle below.

e	t	i	g	r	g
g	e	m	i	b	i
m	n	g	a	i	n
r	t	y	n	m	g
e	l	m	t	e	e
g	e	n	d	e	r

B. Write a list word to finish each sentence.

1. The _____ made the boy ill.

2. The tall bear was a _____

3. The _____ had a lot of room to run and play.

4. The _____ in her ring was shiny blue.

Date: _____

**Lesson 20
Day 3**

gem	ginger	giant
germ	gender	gym

A. Write a list word that matches each definition.

1. A small microbe that causes sickness.

_____

- - - - - - - - - - - - - - - - - - -

_____

2. Condition of being male or female.

_____

- - - - - - - - - - - - - - - - - - -

_____

3. A valuable shiny stone.

_____

- - - - - - - - - - - - - - - - - - -

_____

4. A hot spice.

_____

- - - - - - - - - - - - - - - - - - -

_____

5. Much larger than usual.

_____

- - - - - - - - - - - - - - - - - - -

_____

6. A building for sports.

_____

- - - - - - - - - - - - - - - - - - -

_____

B. Copy the following sentence. **The giant gym was empty**.

_____

- -

_____

- -

_____

- -

_____

gem   ginger   giant
germ   gender   gym

A. Write the list words by adding and subtracting the letters.

sender -s +g   **term -t +g**   **ringer -r +g**

1._____   2._____   3._____

B. Write the list word shown in each picture.

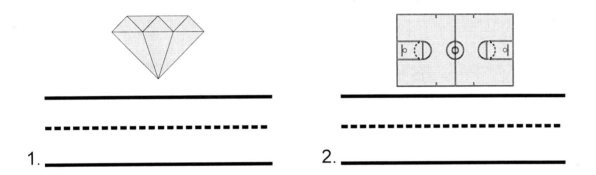

1. _____   2. _____

C. Copy the following sentence. **The giant germ made her sick.**

_____

_____

_____

_____

_____

**Lesson 20
Day 5**

| • Final Test Lesson 21 |

Correction Area:

1. _____   _____

2. _____   _____

3. _____   _____

4. _____   _____

5. _____   _____

6. _____   _____

Carry-over Words   Correction Area

7. _____   _____

8. _____   _____

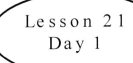

Lesson 21
Day 1

Words with soft **c** sound

1. **Review Your List Words**
   Look at the list words below and read each word to yourself. Then review each definition.

Notice that the beginning **c** in these list words actually makes an **s** sound.

List Words	Definitions
cent	• One penny. One hundredth of one United States dollar.
circle	• A perfectly round shape.
center	• The middle part of something.
circus	• A show that includes clowns, animals, and acrobatic acts.
city	• A place where people live and work. Larger than a town.
celery	• A green plant with stalks that can be eaten.

2. **Take Your Pretest**
   Turn to the next page to the Pretest section and your teacher will ask you to write each list word one at a time.

Pretest - Lesson 21:

Correction Area:

1.

2.

3.

4.

5.

6.

Carry-over Words:

Correction Area:

7.

8.

**Lesson 21
Day 2**

cent	center	city
circle	circus	celery

A. Finish these words.

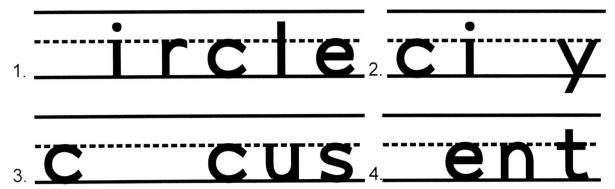

1. _____ircle

2. ci___y

3. c___cus

4. ___ent

B. Write a list word to finish each sentence.

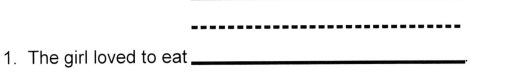

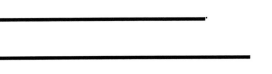

1. The girl loved to eat _____.

2. The courthouse was in the _____ of town.

3. The only money he had was one _____.

4. She drew a _____ around the correct answer.

5. The bigger _____ had taller buildings.

Lesson 21
Day 3

cent	center	city
circle	circus	celery

A. Unscramble the list words.

cntere

1._____

crcius

2._____

clerey

3._____

icrlce

4. **c r e**

tcyi

5._____

etcn

6._____

B. Copy the following sentence. **The circus was in the center of the city.**

Lesson 21
Day 4

cent	center	city
circle	circus	celery

A. Write the list word shown in the picture.

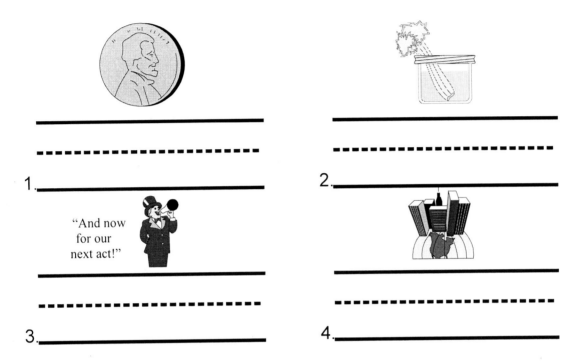

1. _____

2. _____

"And now for our next act!"

3. _____

4. _____

B. Copy the following sentence. **He drew a face in the center of the circle.**

_____

_____

_____

_____

Lesson 21
Day 5

• Final Test Lesson 21

Correction Area:

1.

2.

3.

4.

5.

6.

Carry-over Words

Correction Area

7.

8.

Lesson 22
Day 1

Words with **y** as a vowel

1. Review Your List Words

Look at the list words below and read each word to yourself. Then review each definition.

List Words

fly

pry

sky

spy

my

fry

Definitions

- To move through the air by using wings.

- To open with a long lever.

- The blue dome of air that covers the earth.

- Someone watching in secret.

- Relating to me or myself.

- To cook food in fat or oil.

2. Take Your Pretest

Turn to the next page to the Pretest section and your teacher will ask you to write each list word one at a time.

Date: _____

Pretest - Lesson 22:

1.

2.

3.

4.

5.

6.

Correction Area:

Carry-over Words:

7.

8.

Correction Area:

Level 1, Lesson 22 – Words with **y** as a vowel   128

**Lesson 22
Day 2**

fly	sky	my
pry	spy	fry

A. Write the following list words in alphabetical order.

my, spy, pry

_____   _____   _____

- - - - - - - - - - - - -   - - - - - - - - - - - - -   - - - - - - - - - - - - -

1._____   2._____   3._____

B. Write the list word that matches each definition.

To move through the air
with wings.

_____

- - - - - - - - - - - - -

1. _____

Someone watching
in secret.

_____

- - - - - - - - - - - - -

2. _____

To cook in fat or oil.

_____

- - - - - - - - - - - - -

3. _____

The blue dome that covers
the earth.

_____

- - - - - - - - - - - - -

4. _____

C. Find the list word in each string of letters.

aflyed   bfryd   apryea

_____   _____   _____

- - - - - - - - - - - - -   - - - - - - - - - - - - -   - - - - - - - - - - - - -

1._____   2._____   3._____

Lesson 22
Day 3

fly	sky	my
pry	spy	fry

A. Write a list word to finish each sentence.

_____

1. He likes to _____ on mom in the kitchen.

_____

2. We had to _____ the egg in the skillet.

3. She wanted to _____ in the airplane.

_____

4. She tried to _____ the box open.

B. Copy the following sentence. **In my opinion the sky is blue.**

_____

_____

_____

_____

Lesson 22
Day 4

fly	sky	my
pry	spy	fry

A. Correct the sentences by underlining the word that does not make sense or is spelled incorrectly. Write the correct list word in the space provided.

1. My brother tried to spie on me while I read. _____

2. He needed to prye the lid off the box. _____

3. She wanted to frye the eggs in the pan. _____

4. He wanted to borrow mye skates. _____

B. Copy the following sentence. **He wanted to fly in the sky.**

**Lesson 22
Day 5**

• Final Test Lesson 22

Correction Area:

1. _____

2. _____

3. _____

4. _____

5. _____

6. _____

Carry-over Words

Correction Area

7. _____

8. _____

**Lesson 23
Day 1**

Words with **oo** sound

1. **Review Your List Words**
   Look at the list words below and read each word to yourself. Then review each definition.

   This is known as a **digraph**, which is two vowels placed side by side that act together to make one vowel sound.

   Notice that this particular **oo** digraph is capable of making three different sounds: 1) the vowel sound you hear in the word **book**, 2) the vowel sound you hear in the word **moon**, and 3) the vowel sound you hear in the word **flood**.

   There is no particular rule to follow in determining which sound an **oo** digraph makes. Practice makes perfect here!

List Words	Definitions
moon	• The celestial body that orbits the earth.
spoon	• An eating utensil with a small bowl and a handle.
book	• Sheets of paper with writing that are bound together.
cook	• To prepare food for eating by using heat.
blood	• A red liquid that circulates oxygen through an animal or human body.
flood	• To become overfilled with water.

2. **Take Your Pretest**
   Turn to the next page to the Pretest section and your teacher will ask you to write each list word one at a time.

Pretest - Lesson 23:   Correction Area:

1. _____   _____

2. _____   _____

3. _____   _____

4. _____   _____

5. _____   _____

6. _____   _____

Carry-over Words: Correction Area:

7. _____   _____

8. _____   _____

Lesson 23
Day 2

| moon | book | blood |
| spoon | cook | flood |

A. Match list words that have the same **oo** sound by drawing lines to connect each pair.

moon   cook

flood   spoon

book   blood

B. Write the list word that matches each definition.

Celestial body that orbits the earth.   To overfill with water.

1. _____   2. _____

Prepare food with heat.   An eating utensil.

3. _____   4. _____

C. Find the list word in each string of letters.

emooni   nsbooke   tbloode

1. _____   2. _____   3. _____

**Lesson 23
Day 3**

moon	book	blood
spoon	cook	flood

A. Write a list word to finish each sentence.

1. He used a _____ to eat his soup.

2. There was some red _____ from his cut.

3. The full _____ was bright and shiny in the sky.

4. There was a _____ after two days of heavy rain.

B. Copy the following sentence. **He read a book on how to cook.**

_____

_____

_____

_____

Lesson 23
Day 4

moon	book	blood
spoon	cook	flood

A. Write the list word shown in the picture.

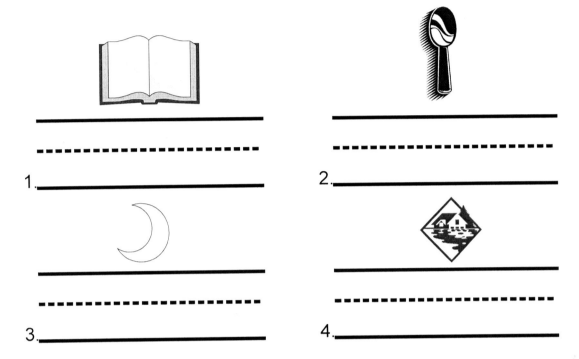

1. _____

2. _____

3. _____

4. _____

B. Copy the following sentence. **The cook cut her finger and saw blood.**

_____

_____

_____

_____

**Lesson 23
Day 5**

• Final Test Lesson 23

Correction Area:

1.

2.

3.

4.

5.

6.

Carry-over Words   Correction Area

7.

8.

Level 1, Lesson 23 – Words with **oo** sound   138

Lesson 24 Review Day 1

Review of words with long vowel **o** sound using **ow**

List Words

low	bow	row	mow	bowl	snow

A. Underline each list word spelled incorrectly and write it correctly below.

1. He shot an arrow with his boew.

2. Her bole was full of food.

3. The water in the tank was lowe.

4. They like to rowe the boat.

5. It was time to moew the lawn.

6. The sno was cold on her tongue.

B. Write the above list words in alphabetical order.

1. _____

2. **bowl**

3. _____

4. _____

5. _____

6. _____

Date: _____

Review of words with soft **g** sound

List Words

gem	germ	ginger	gender	giant	gym

A. Correct the sentences by underlining the word that does not make sense and replace it with a list word.

_____

- - - - - - - - - - - - - - - - -

1. He washed his hands to get rid of the jerm. _____

_____

- -

2. The spicy meat was flavored with jinger. _____.

_____

- - - - - - - - - - - - - - - -

3. The gendre of the rabbit was male. _____

_____

- - - - - - - - - - - - - - - - -

4. The jem was bright and shiny. _____

_____

- - - - - - - - - - - - - - - -

5. They went to the jim to play sports. _____

_____

- - - - - - - - - - - - - - - -

6. The gyant dog was the largest he had seen. _____

Lesson 24
Review
Day 3

Review of words with soft **c** sound

List Words

| cent | circle | center | circus | city | celery |

A. Read each word below. If there is a list word that rhymes with the given word, write it below. Otherwise, write **none**.

bent

_____

- - - - - - - - - - - - - - - - -

1._____

cut

_____

- - - - - - - - - - - - - - - - -

2._____

pity

_____

- - - - - - - - - - - - - - - - -

3._____

B. Read the definitions and write the correct list word below.

1. The middle part of something.

_____

- - - - - - - - - - - - - - - - - - -

_____

2. Larger than a town.

3. A show that has clowns and acrobats.

_____

- - - - - - - - - - - - - - - - - - -

_____

4. A round shape.

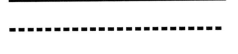

5. A green plant with stalks.

_____

- - - - - - - - - - - - - - - - - - -

_____

6. One penny.

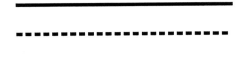

Lesson 24
Review
Day 4

Review of words with **y** as a vowel

List Words

fly	pry	sky	spy	my	fry

A. Write a list word to finish each sentence.

_____

1. He wanted to _____ his food in the pan.

_____

2. She sat in _____ chair.

_____

3. The _____ hid in the shadows.

_____

4. He had to _____the lid off of the crate.

B. Write two list words that begin with the letter **s**.

1. _____   2. _____

C. Write two list words that begin with the letter **f**.

1. _____   2. _____

Lesson 24
Review
Day 5

Review of words with **oo** sound

List Words

| moon | spoon | book | cook | blood | flood |

A. Find and circle each list word in the puzzle below.

b	o	o	k	m	e
o	n	c	s	o	b
n	e	o	t	o	l
s	p	o	o	n	o
b	g	k	x	f	o
o	f	l	o	o	d

B. Unscramble and write the list words.

1. flodo

2. npsoo

3. odolb

4. noom

5. kboo

6. kooc

<<Intentionally left blank>>

Lesson 25
Day 1

Words with **ir**

1. **Review Your List Words**
   Look at the list words below and read each word to yourself. Then review each definition.

List Words

| bird |
| dirt |
| stir |
| girl |
| firm |
| skirt |

Definitions

- A feathered animal with wings that lays eggs.

- Soil that makes up a part of the earth's surface.

- To mix something up.

- A female child.

- Something that is strong or solid.

- A girl's garment that hangs from the waist down and does not have legs.

2. **Take Your Pretest**
   Turn to the next page to the Pretest section and your teacher will ask you to write each list word one at a time.

Pretest - Lesson 25:   Correction Area:

1.

2.

3.

4.

5.

6.

Carry-over Words: Correction Area:

7.

8.

Date: _____

Lesson 25
Day 2

| bird | stir | firm |
| dirt | girl | skirt |

A. Write the list words you see in each sentence.

The bird built a firm nest.

_____

- - - - - - - - - - - - - - - - -   - - - - - - - - - - - - - - - - -

1. _____   2. _____

The girl got dirt on her skirt.

_____

- - - - - - - - - - - - - - - - -   - - - - - - - - - - - - - - - - -

3. _____   4. _____

_____

- - - - - - - - - - - - - - - - -

5. _____

B. Write a list word to finish each sentence.

_____

- -

1. The _____ soars in the sky.

_____

- -

2. The girl played outside in the _____.

_____

- - - - - - - - - - - - - - - - - -

3. She had to _____ the pot on the stove.

Lesson 25
Day 3

bird	stir	firm
dirt	girl	skirt

A. Finish these words.

1.  __rd 2. s__rt

3. s__r 4. d__t

5. g__ 6. f__m

B. Copy the following sentence. **The bird built a firm nest with dirt.**

Lesson 25
Day 4

bird	stir	firm
dirt	girl	skirt

A. Write the list word shown in the picture.

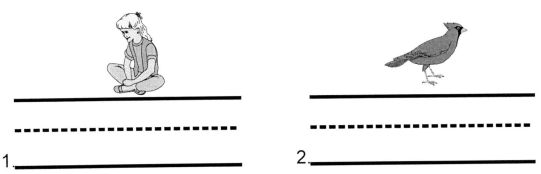

1. _____

2. _____

B. Find the list word in each string of letters.

askirto   **odirted**   **sfirmn**

1. _____   2. _____   3. _____

C. Copy the following sentence. **The girl in the skirt had to stir the pot.**

Lesson 25
Day 5

- Final Test Lesson 25

Correction Area:

1. _____

2. _____

3. _____

4. _____

5. _____

6. _____

Carry-over Words

Correction Area

7. _____

8. _____

**Lesson 26
Day 1**

Words with **er**

1. Review Your List Words
Look at the list words below and read each word to yourself. Then review each definition.

List Words	Definitions
jerk	• To pull in a quick powerful motion.
clerk	• A salesperson in a store. Also, one who keeps records.
her	• Something related to a female.
fern	• A green plant that has pointy divided leaves.
herd	• A group of animals.
term	• A fixed period of time.

2. Take Your Pretest
Turn to the next page to the Pretest section and your teacher will ask you to write each list word one at a time.

Pretest - Lesson 26:

Correction Area:

1.

2.

3.

4.

5.

6.

Carry-over Words:

Correction Area:

7.

8.

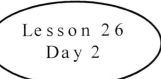

Lesson 26
Day 2

jerk	her	herd
clerk	fern	term

A. Find and circle each list word in the puzzle below.

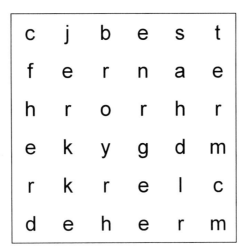

B. Write the word in each set of words that comes first in the alphabet.

her, fern, herd   term, jerk, herd   fern, her, clerk

_____   _____   _____

- - - - - - - - - - - -   - - - - - - - - - - - -   - - - - - - - - - - - -

1. _____   2. _____   3. _____

C. Write a list word to finish each sentence.

_____

- - - - - - - - - - - - -

1. She had to _____ her rope quickly to lasso the calf.

_____

- -

2. The president has a _____ of four years.

_____

- - - - - - - - - - - - -

3. The store _____ waited on the customers.

Lesson 26
Day 3

jerk	her	herd
clerk	fern	term

A. Finish these words.

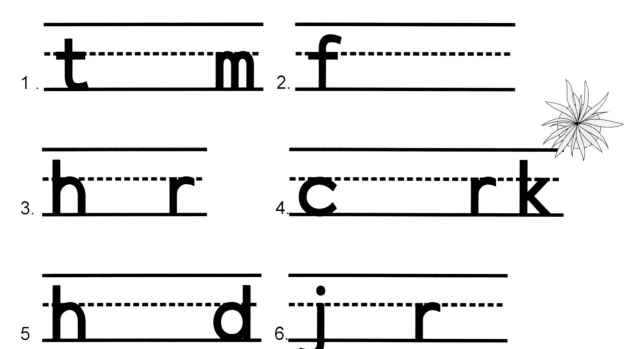

1. t _____ m

2. f _____

3. h _____ r

4. c _____ r k

5. h _____ d

6. j _____ r

B. Copy the following sentence. **She fed her hungry herd of bison.**

Lesson 26
Day 4

| jerk | her | herd |
| clerk | fern | term |

A. Read each definition and write the correct list word below.

1. To pull in a quick motion.

_____

_____

2. A green plant with pointy leaves.

_____

_____

3. A group of animals.

_____

_____

4. A fixed period of time.

_____

_____

5. Relating to a girl.

_____

_____

6. A person who keeps records.

_____

_____

B. Copy the following sentence. **She handed her fern to the clerk.**

_____

_____

_____

Lesson 26
Day 5

• Final Test Lesson 26

Correction Area:

1.

2.

3.

4.

5.

6.

Carry-over Words

Correction Area

7.

8.

Words with **ur**

1. **Review Your List Words**
   Look at the list words below and read each word to yourself. Then review each definition.

List Words	Definitions
turn	• To change direction.
burn	• To be on fire. Destroyed by heat.
purse	• A storage bag usually carried by women. A handbag.
nurse	• A person skilled in caring for the sick.
urn	• A vase that usually rests on a stand.
urban	• Related to being in a city.

2. **Take Your Pretest**
   Turn to the next page to the Pretest section and your teacher will ask you to write each list word one at a time.

Pretest - Lesson 27:   Correction Area:

1. _____   _____

2. _____   _____

3. _____   _____

4. _____   _____

5. _____   _____

6. _____   _____

Carry-over Words: Correction Area:

7. _____   _____

8. _____   _____

Lesson 27
Day 2

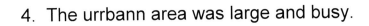

turn	purse	urn
burn	nurse	urban

A. Underline the list words in the following sentences that are spelled incorrectly.

1. The car made a quick tern away from the storm.

2. The lady had a pretty perse around her arm.

3. The urne held a nice plant.

4. The urrbann area was large and busy.

5. The nerse took good care of the sick person.

6. The man had a brun from staying outside in the sun too long.

B. Correctly write the above list words that are misspelled.

1. _____   2. _____   3. _____

4. _____   5. _____   6. _____

C. Write a list word to describe each picture.

1. _____   2. _____

Level 1, Lesson 27 – Words with **ur**

159

Lesson 27
Day 3

turn	purse	urn
burn	nurse	urban

A. Finish these words.

1.  n _____ s

2. t _____ n

3. b _____ n

4. _____ b a

5. u _____ n

6. p _____ r

B. Copy the following sentence. **The nurse cared for the patient with a burn.**

Lesson 27
Day 4

turn	purse	urn
burn	nurse	urban

A. Read each definition and write the correct list word below.

1. To be on fire.

_____

_ _ _ _ _ _ _ _ _ _ _ _ _ _

_____

2. To change direction.

_____

_ _ _ _ _ _ _ _ _ _ _ _ _ _

_____

3. A person skilled in taking care of the sick.

_____

_ _ _ _ _ _ _ _ _ _ _ _ _ _

_____

4. Relating to being in a city.

_____

_ _ _ _ _ _ _ _ _ _ _ _ _ _

_____

5. A vase.

_____

_ _ _ _ _ _ _ _ _ _ _ _ _ _

_____

6. A handbag.

_____

_ _ _ _ _ _ _ _ _ _ _ _ _ _

_____

B. Copy the following sentence. **The urn would not fit into her purse.**

_____

_ _

_____

_ _

_____

_ _

_____

Lesson 27
Day 5

• Final Test Lesson 27

Correction Area:

1.

2.

3.

4.

5.

6.

Carry-over Words

Correction Area

7.

8.

Lesson 28
Day 1

| Words with **or** |

1. **Review Your List Words**
   Look at the list words below and read each word to yourself. Then review each definition.

List Words   **Definitions**

| worm | • A soft-bodied creeping animal. |

| work | • To use one's ability to get something done. |

| world | • The earth. |

| worse | • Something that is not as good in comparison to something else. |

| worth | • Giving value to something. |

| word | • A combination of letters that means something. |

2. **Take Your Pretest**
   Turn to the next page to the Pretest section and your teacher will ask you to write each list word one at a time.

Pretest - Lesson 28:   Correction Area:

1. _____   _____

2. _____   _____

3. _____   _____

4. _____   _____

5. _____   _____

6. _____   _____

Carry-over Words: Correction Area:

7. _____   _____

8. _____   _____

Lesson 28
Day 2

worm	world	worth
work	worse	word

A. Underline the list words in the following sentences that are spelled incorrectly.

1. The men made quick werk of the pile of boxes.

2. The first play was werse than the second play.

3. She used a funny worde to describe her brother.

4. The werme crawled across the yard.

5. He was the smartest boy in the wearld.

6. The painting was werth more than she thought.

B. Correctly write the above list words that are misspelled.

1._____ 2._____ 3._____

4._____ 5._____ 6._____

C. Write a list word that describes each picture.

1. _____ 2._____

Date: _____

Lesson 28 Day 3

worm	world	worth
work	worse	word

A. Unscramble the list words.

swreo

_____

1._____

thorw

_____

2._____

krow

_____

3._____

wrdo

_____

4._____

rmow

_____

5._____

ldowr

_____

6._____

B. Copy the following sentence. **It is worth less than he thought.**

_____

_____

_____

**Lesson 28
Day 4**

worm	world	worth
work	worse	word

A. Read each definition and write the correct list word below.

1. The earth.

2. Giving value to something.

3. To use one's ability to get something done.

4. Not as good as something else.

5. A soft-bodied creeping animal.

6. A combination of letters that mean something.

B. Copy the following sentence. **He had to work since he gave his word.**

Lesson 28
Day 5

| Final Test Lesson 28 |

Correction Area:

1. _____

2. _____

3. _____

4. _____

5. _____

6. _____

Carry-over Words

Correction Area

7. _____

8. _____

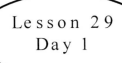

Lesson 29
Day 1

Words with **ear**

1. Review Your List Words

Look at the list words below and read each word to yourself. Then review each definition.

List Words

| earth |
| search |
| earn |
| heard |
| learn |
| yearn |

Definitions

- The third planet from the sun. The planet on which we live.

- To look for something.

- To receive money for work performed.

- To receive noise by the ear. Past tense of hear.

- To gain skill by practice or study.

- A desire or craving for something.

2. Take Your Pretest

Turn to the next page to the Pretest section and your teacher will ask you to write each list word one at a time.

Pretest - Lesson 29:   Correction Area:

1.

2.

3.

4.

5.

6.

Carry-over Words: Correction Area:

7.

8.

Lesson 29
Day 2

| earth   earn   learn |
| search heard yearn |

A. Put the following list words in alphabetical order.

earn, yearn, search

1._____ 2._____ 3._____

B. Read the following sentence and write the list words you see.

He heard that the assignment was to learn about the earth.

1._____ 2._____ 3._____

C. Underline the list words in the following sentences that are spelled incorrectly.

1. The boys yuearn to eat some ice cream.

2. He had to serche for the missing cookie.

3. The erth is the planet on which we live.

4. The class had to larne how to spell.

5. She mowed the lawn to ern money for a bicycle.

6. They herde the cows mooing in the barn.

Lesson 29
Day 3

| earth | earn | learn |
| search | heard | yearn |

A. Unscramble the list words.

threa

_____

1._____

aern

_____

2._____

yrean

_____

3._____

haerd

_____

4._____

serach

_____

5._____

lrnea

_____

6._____

B. Copy the following sentence. **He had to learn how to earn money.**

_____

_____

_____

_____

Lesson 29
Day 4

| earth | earn | learn |
| search | heard | yearn |

A. Read each definition and write the correct list word below.

1. To gain skill by study
   or practice.

   _____

   - - - - - - - - - - - - - - - - - -

   _____

2. To receive money for work
   performed.

   _____

   - - - - - - - - - - - - - - - - - -

   _____

3. The planet on which we live.

   _____

   - - - - - - - - - - - - - - - - - -

   _____

4. A desire for something.

   _____

   - - - - - - - - - - - - - - - - - -

   _____

5. To look for something.

   _____

   - - - - - - - - - - - - - - - - - -

   _____

6. To receive noise by your ears.

   _____

   - - - - - - - - - - - - - - - - - -

   _____

B. Copy the following sentence. **She heard that the earth was round.**

_____

- -

_____

_____

- -

_____

_____

- -

_____

**Lesson 29
Day 5**

• Final Test Lesson 29

Correction Area:

1.

2.

3.

4.

5.

6.

Carry-over Words

Correction Area

7.

8.

Lesson 30
Review
Day 1

Review of words with **ir**

List Words

| bird | dirt | stir | girl | firm | skirt |

A. Underline each list word spelled incorrectly and write them below.

1. He got dert on his pants.

_____

_____

2. The burd flew in the sky.

_____

_____

3. The gurl read a book.

_____

_____

4. The concrete wall was ferm.

_____

_____

5. It was time to ster the bowl.

_____

_____

6. Her skeart was trimmed in lace.

_____

_____

B. Write the above list words in alphabetical order.

_____   _____   _____

1._____   2._____   3._____

_____   _____

4._____   5._____   6. **stir**

**Lesson 30
Review
Day 2**

Review of words with **er**

List Words

| jerk | clerk | her | fern | herd | term |

A. Find the list word in each string of letters. Write them below.

aejerki

therdp

dherz

1._____ 2._____ 3._____

aclerkd

tterma

nfernb

4._____ 5._____ 6._____

B. Match the list word with its definition. Draw a line to connect each pair.

her   A group of like animals living together.

clerk   A green leafy plant with pointy leafs.

jerk   Related to a female.

term   A limited period of time.

herd   A person who keeps records.

fern   To pull quickly.

Lesson 30
Review
Day 3

Review of words with **ur**

List Words

| turn | burn | purse | nurse | urn | urban |

A. Write the three list words that end with the letters **urn**.

1._____ 2._____ 3._____

B. Read each definition and write the correct list word below.

1. A person who cares for the sick.

2. To be on fire.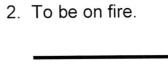

3. To change direction.

4. A bag carried by a woman.

5. A vase that sits on a stand.

6. Something related to a city.

Lesson 30 Review Day 4

Review of words with **or**

List Words

worm	work	world	worse	worth	word

A. Write a list word to finish each sentence. Use each list word only once.

1. The king wanted to rule the _____.

2. The old couch was _____ very little money.

3. The lady had to _____ for money.

4. The first book was _____than the last book.

B. Underline the list words in each sentence.

1. He wanted to spell the word correctly.

2. The worm moved through the grass.

3. The world is large and round.

4. The old coin was worth a lot of money.

5. The spelling test was worse than he thought.

Lesson 30
Review
Day 5

Review of words with **ear**

List Words

earth	search	earn	heard	learn	yearn

A. Unscramble and write the list words.

1. aern

2. lrnea

3. hrdea

4. sercha

5. erath

6. yeran

B. Finish these words.

1.  s ____ ch

2.  e ____ n

3.  ____ rth

4.  l ____ arn

5. 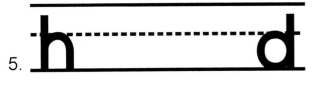 h ____ d

6. 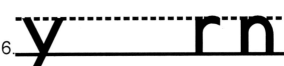 y ____ rn

<<Intentionally left blank>>

Lesson 31
Day 1

Words with beginning
s blend **st**

1. **Review Your List Words**
   Look at the list words below and read each word to yourself. Then review each definition.

List Words	Definitions
stay	• To remain in one place.
step	• The height of one stair.
star	• A celestial body which is visible at night as a light in the sky.
stem	• The stalk of a plant.
stop	• To end or finish.
study	• To learn by reading.

2. **Take Your Pretest**
   Turn to the next page to the Pretest section and your teacher will ask you to write each list word one at a time.

Pretest - Lesson 31:

Correction Area:

1.

2.

3.

4.

5.

6.

Carry-over Words:

Correction Area:

7.

8.

Lesson 31
Day 2

| stay | star | stop |
| step | stem | study |

A. Look at each picture. Write the List Word that matches the picture.

1. _____   2. _____   3. _____

B. Write the list words by adding and subtracting the letters.

car -c +st   hay -h +st   hop -h +st

1. _____   2. _____   3. _____

yep -y +st   gem -g +st   sturdy -r

4. _____   5. _____   6. _____

C. Write the two list words that end with a **p**.

1. _____   2. _____

Lesson 31
Day 3

| stay | star | stop |
| step | stem | study |

A. Unscramble the list words.

teps

1._____

tsme

2._____

ydtsu

3._____

rats

4._____

syta

5._____

pots

6._____

B. Copy the following sentence. **He had to stay on the step to study the star.**

Lesson 31
Day 4

| stay | star | stop |
| step | stem | study |

A. Read each definition and write the correct list word below.

1. To remain in one place.

_____

- - - - - - - - - - - - - - - - -

_____

2. A celestial body.

_____

- - - - - - - - - - - - - - - - -

_____

3. To end or finish.

_____

- - - - - - - - - - - - - - - - -

_____

4. The stalk of a plant.

_____

- - - - - - - - - - - - - - - - -

_____

5. The height of one stair.

_____

- - - - - - - - - - - - - - - - -

_____

6. To learn by reading.

_____

- - - - - - - - - - - - - - - - -

_____

B. Copy the following sentence. **She wanted to stop and study the plant stem.**

_____

- -

_____

- -

_____

- -

_____

Lesson 31
Day 5

| Final Test Lesson 31 |

Correction Area:

1. _____

2. _____

3. _____

4. _____

5. _____

6. _____

Carry-over Words   Correction Area

7. _____

8. _____

Level 1, Lesson 31 – Words with beginning **s** blends **st**   186

Lesson 32
Day 1

Words with beginning
s blend sl

1. **Review Your List Words**
   Look at the list words below and read each word to yourself. Then review each definition.

List Words	Definitions
slow	• Moving at less than normal speed.
slip	• To slide into or out of place.
sled	• A vessel built on skis or runners made to travel over snow.
slam	• A noisy, fast closing.
sleep	• An inactive state where the body rests.
slot	• A narrow, rectangular opening.

2. **Take Your Pretest**
   Turn to the next page to the Pretest section and your teacher will ask you to write each list word one at a time.

Date: _____

Pretest - Lesson 32:

Correction Area:

1. _____

2. _____

3. _____

4. _____

5. _____

6. _____

Carry-over Words:

Correction Area:

7. _____

8. _____

Lesson 32
Day 2

slow	sled	sleep
slip	slam	slot

A. Underline the list words in the following sentences that are spelled incorrectly. Write each list word correctly below.

_____

----

1. I told him not to slaam the door. _____

_____

----

2. She put the letter in the mail box slotte. _____

_____

----

3. He was tired, but it was hard to slep. _____

_____

----

4. The water on the floor made him sllip. _____

_____

----

5. She went down the snowy hill on the sledd. _____

_____

----

6. The injured horse walked at a sllow pace. _____

B. Unscramble the list words.

selpe   lwos   dles

_____

1._____ 2._____ 3._____

Lesson 32
Day 3

slow	sled	sleep
slip	slam	slot

A. Unscramble the list words.

masl

lseep

_____

_____

- - - - - - - - - - - - - - - - - -

- - - - - - - - - - - - - - - - - -

1. _____

2. _____

lips

wlos

_____

_____

- - - - - - - - - - - - - - - - - -

- - - - - - - - - - - - - - - - - -

3. _____

4. _____

tosl

leds

_____

_____

- - - - - - - - - - - - - - - - - -

- - - - - - - - - - - - - - - - - -

5. _____

6. _____

B. Copy the following sentence. **He had to slip the coin into the slot.**

_____

- -

_____

_____

- -

_____

_____

- -

_____

slow	sled	sleep
slip	slam	slot

A. Match the list word to each given definition.

slam   A vessel that travels on snow.

slot   Moving at less than normal speed.

slip   To slide into or out of place.

sleep   A noisy, fast closing.

slow   A narrow opening.

sled   An inactive state where the body rests.

B. Copy the following sentence. **The sled was slow in the deep snow.**

Lesson 32
Day 5

• Final Test Lesson 32

Correction Area:

1. _____

2. _____

3. _____

4. _____

5. _____

6. _____

Carry-over Words   Correction Area

7. _____

8. _____

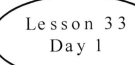

Lesson 33
Day 1

Words with beginning
s blend sn

1. **Review Your List Words**
   Look at the list words below and read each word to yourself. Then
   review each definition.

Word List	Definitions

Word List

snout

snip

snoop

snore

snug

snap

Definitions

- A long nose that sticks out from the face. Like a pig's nose.

- To cut a small piece away with scissors.

- To look or search in a sneaky way.

- A rough noise that occurs while sleeping.

- Something that fits tightly.

- A quick, loud clicking noise. A two-piece device which connects to hold something together.

2. **Take Your Pretest**
   Turn to the next page to the Pretest section and your teacher will ask you
   to write each list word one at a time.

Pretest - Lesson 33:   Correction Area:

1.

2.

3.

4.

5.

6.

Carry-over Words: Correction Area:

7.

8.

Lesson 33
Day 2

snout	snoop	snug
snip	snore	snap

A. Write the two list words that mean to make some kind of sound or noise.

1._____ 2._____

B. Write the list word that matches each definition.

1. Something that fits tightly. _____

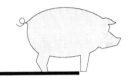

2. A long nose that sticks out from the face. _____

3. To look in a sneaky way. _____

4. To cut a small piece away. _____

5. A rough noise that occurs during sleep. _____

snout	snoop	snug
snip	snore	snap

A. Underline the list word spelled incorrectly and write it correctly below.

1. The snoot of the pig was long.

2. The cap made a snapp.

3. She will snoor as she sleeps.

4. He liked to snoope around.

5. She had to snnip off some paper.

6. The new socks were snuge.

B. Copy the following sentence. **He could barely snap the snug coat.**

Date: _____

Lesson 33
Day 4

snout	snoop	snug
snip	snore	snap

A. Read the following sentences and underline the words with the **sn** sound. Write the list words you find.

While being a snoop, he could barely snap his coat since it was snug.

1. _____ 2. _____ 3. _____

The rabbit ate a snip of grass before falling asleep to snore.

4. _____ 5. _____

B. Copy the following sentence. **The pig used his snout to snoop around.**

_____

_____

_____

_____

Level 1, Lesson 33 – Words with beginning **s** blend **sn**

Lesson 33
Day 5

• Final Test Lesson 33

Correction Area:

1.

2.

3.

4.

5.

6.

Carry-over Words   Correction Area

7.

8.

Lesson 34
Day 1

Words with beginning
s blend sk

1. Review Your List Words
Look at the word list below and read each word to yourself. Then review each definition.

List Words	Definitions
skip	• Brisk movement by hopping and stepping.
skim	• To pass lightly over something.
skit	• A brief play put on by actors.
skin	• The outer layer of an animal's body.
ski	• To glide over the snow on skis.
skate	• A shoe or boot with an attached blade used for gliding over ice.

2. Take Your Pretest
Turn to the next page to the Pretest section and your teacher will ask you to write each list word one at a time.

Pretest - Lesson 34:   Correction Area:

1.

2.

3.

4.

5.

6.

Carry-over Words: Correction Area:

7.

8.

skip	skit	ski
skim	skin	skate

A. Write the list word that does not contain the letter **i**.

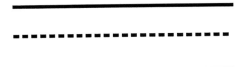

B. Write the word that matches each definition.

1. A shoe with an attached blade used to glide over ice.

2. To glide over the snow on skis.

3. The outer layer of an animal's body.

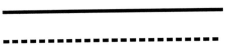

4. Brisk movement by hopping or stepping.

5. A brief play put on by actors.

**Lesson 34
Day 3**

skip	skit	ski
skim	skin	skate

A. Underline the list word spelled incorrectly and write it correctly below.

1. He wanted to skii on the snow.

   _____

   - - - - - - - - - - - - - - -

   _____

2. The girl's skinn was red.

   _____

   - - - - - - - - - - - - - - -

   _____

3. She will skyp all the way home.

   _____

   - - - - - - - - - - - - - - -

   _____

4. The bug could skiim the surface of the water.

   _____

   - - - - - - - - - - - - - - -

   _____

5. They acted in a funny skitt.

   _____

   - - - - - - - - - - - - - - -

   _____

6. The skat glided across the ice.

   _____

   - - - - - - - - - - - - - - -

   _____

B. Copy the following sentence. **She had to skip during the skit.**

_____

- -

_____

_____

- -

_____

_____

- -

_____

Lesson 34
Day 4

| skip | skit | ski |
| skim | skin | skate |

A. Unscramble the list words.

ipsk

1._____

teksa

2._____

ksi

3._____

tiks

4._____

kmis

5._____

skni

6._____

B. Copy the following sentence. **She used a ski or skate to skim across the snow.**

Date: _____

• Final Test Lesson 34

Correction Area:

1.

2.

3.

4.

5.

6.

Carry-over Words   Correction Area

7.

8.

Lesson 35
Day 1

Words with beginning
s blend sp

1. **Review Your List Words**
   Look at the list words below and read each word to yourself. Then review each definition.

   List Words   **Definitions**

space	• The area beyond the earth's atmosphere.
spare	• An extra. Having more than you need in reserve.
spent	• All used up, no more available.
spin	• A rapid twisting or rotating motion.
spell	• To arrange letters in the correct order to form a word.
spill	• To cause or allow a substance to run or fall out of a container.

2. **Take Your Pretest**
   Turn to the next page to the Pretest section and your teacher will ask you to write each list word one at a time.

Date: _____

Pretest - Lesson 35:   Correction Area:

1.

2.

3.

4.

5.

6.

Carry-over Words: Correction Area:

7.

8.

Lesson 35
Day 2

| space | spent | spell |
| spare | spin | spill |

A. Find and circle each list word in the puzzle below.

s	n	i	p	s	s
s	p	e	l	p	p
e	p	a	d	a	e
l	v	i	c	r	n
n	i	e	l	e	t
s	p	e	l	l	x

B. Unscramble the list words.

1. psin _____

2. pasce _____

3. lepsl _____

4. pilsl _____

5. entps _____

6. spera _____

C. Write the two list words that have a short **i** sound.

1. _____

2. _____

**Lesson 35
Day 3**

space	spent	spell
spare	spin	spill

A. Write the list words by adding and subtracting the letters. (Replace the letter from the same place where it was subtracted.)

face -f +sp   fin -f +sp   fill -f +sp

1._____ 2._____ 3._____

care -c +sp   cent -c +sp   bell -b +sp

4._____ 5._____ 6._____

B. Copy the following sentence. **She spent her spare money.**

Lesson 35
Day 4

| space | spent | spell |
| spare | spin | spill |

A. Write a list word to complete each sentence.

1. She likes to _____ the colorful top.

2. Did you _____ the water on the floor?

3. He _____ all of his money.

4. She learned to _____ all of her list words correctly.

B. Copy the following sentence. **We saw the spare rocket spin in space.**

Lesson 35
Day 5

• Final Test Lesson 35

Correction Area:

1.

2.

3.

4.

5.

6.

Carry-over Words   Correction Area

7.

8.

**Lesson 36
Review
Day 1**

Review of words with beginning s blend **st**

List Words

stay	step	star	stem	stop	study

A. Underline the list word spelled incorrectly and write it correctly below.

1. He had to stuidy for the test.

_____

- -

_____

2. They came to a stopp at the sign.

_____

- -

_____

3. The stemm of the plant was green and tall.

_____

- -

_____

4. The stepp was going upward.

_____

- -

_____

5. The staar was bright in the sky.

_____

- -

_____

6. He had to sstay at home.

_____

- -

_____

B. Write the list words by adding and subtracting the letters. (Replace the letter from the same place where it was subtracted.)

play – pl +st

_____

- - - - - - - - - - - - - -

1._____

stew – w +p

_____

- - - - - - - - - - - - - -

2._____

far – f +st

_____

- - - - - - - - - - - - - -

3._____

step – p +m

_____

- - - - - - - - - - - - - -

4._____

hop – h +st

_____

- - - - - - - - - - - - - -

5._____

steady – ea +u

_____

- - - - - - - - - - - - - -

6._____

Lesson 36
Review
Day 2

Review of words with beginning s blend sl

List Words

slow	slip	sled	slam	sleep	slot

A. Find and write the list word in each string of letters.

aslede

1. _____

hslipd

2. _____

tsleepn

3. _____

slamis

4. _____

nslote

5. _____

tslowr

6. _____

B. Read each definition and write the correct list word below.

1. Moving at less than normal speed.

2. A narrow rectangular opening.

3. To slide into or out of place.

4. Inactive state when the body rests.

5. A vessel that travels over snow.

6. Noisy fast closing.

Lesson 36
Review
Day 3

**Review of words with beginning
s blend sn**

List Words

| snout | snip | snoop | snore | snug | snap |

A. Read each word below and write a list word that rhymes.

scout
_____
- - - - - - - - - - - - - - - -
1._____

trip
_____
- - - - - - - - - - - - - - - -
2._____

trap
_____
- - - - - - - - - - - - - - - -
3._____

loop
_____
- - - - - - - - - - - - - - - -
4._____

chore
_____
- - - - - - - - - - - - - - - -
5._____

chug
_____
- - - - - - - - - - - - - - - -
6._____

B. Match the list word with its definition. Draw a line to connect each pair.

snoop   A short quick sound.

snout   To sneak in silence.

snug   A noise while you sleep.

snap   A bit too small.

snore   To take a small piece.

snip   A long nose that sticks out.

Lesson 36
Review
Day 4

Review of words with beginning s blend sk

List Words

| skip | skim | skit | skin | ski | skate |

A. Write a list word to finish each sentence.

_____

- - - - - - - - - - - - - - - - - - -

1. We love to _____ down the snow covered slope.

_____

- - - - - - - - - - - - - - - - - - - -

2. She loved to _____ happily down the sidewalk.

_____

- - - - - - - - - - - - - - - - -

3. The bug can _____ across the water's surface.

_____

- - - - - - - - - - - - - - - - - - -

4. Her _____ was tan after being in the sun.

_____

- - - - - - - - - - - - - - - - - - - -

5. They acted out a very funny _____.

_____

- - - - - - - - - - - - - - - - - - - -

6. The hockey player loved to _____ on the ice.

**Lesson 36
Review
Day 5**

Review of words with beginning
s blends **sp**

List Words

space	spare	spent	spin	spell	spill

A. Unscramble and write the list words.

1. asper

_____
- - - - - - - - - - - - - -
_____

2. llspe

_____
- - - - - - - - - - - - - -
_____

3. sipll

_____
- - - - - - - - - - - - - -
_____

4. stenp

_____
- - - - - - - - - - - - - -
_____

5. sinp

_____
- - - - - - - - - - - - - -
_____

6. ecaps

_____
- - - - - - - - - - - - - -
_____

B. Finish these words.

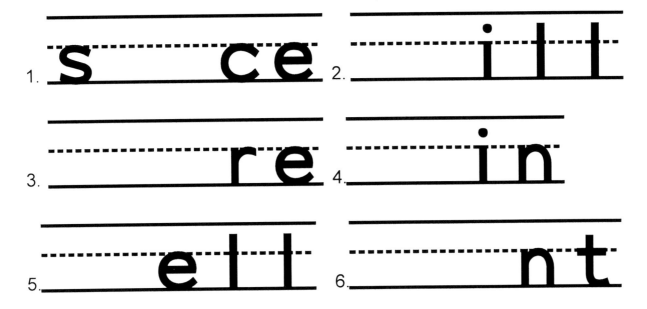

1. s_____ce   2. _____ill

3. _____re   4. _____in

5. _____ell   6. _____nt

The Alphabet

The below 26 letters make up the English alphabet. You will notice that there are two letters on each line. The taller letter on each line is called the **capital** letter (For example: A). Another name for a capital letter is an uppercase letter. Each shorter letter is called a lower case letter (For example: a). Notice how the uppercase letter touches the top of the line while the lowercase letter does not. The letters below are arranged in alphabetical order.

Aa Bb Cc Dd

Ee Ff Gg Hh

Ii Jj Kk Ll

Mm Nn Oo Pp

Qq Rr Ss Tt

Uu Vv Ww Xx

Yy Zz

Using the Dictionary

Learning to use the **dictionary** is an important skill. A dictionary shows how to spell words and how to say them. It also tells the meaning of each word. The words in the dictionary are called **entry words**.

Kitten (kit-en) a young cat.

The letters in parentheses tell you how to pronounce the entry word **kitten**. There is sometimes more than one pronunciation for a word.

Ketchup (kech'*up*, kach'*up*) a thick spicy sauce made with tomatoes.

The group of words after the parentheses is the definition, which tells what the word means.

The first step to finding a word in the dictionary is to find the section of the dictionary in which the word will be found. Words that start with **A, B, C, D, E, F,** or **G**, are found near the **front** part of the dictionary. Words that start with **H, I, J, K, L, M, N, O,** or **P**, are found near the **middle** of the dictionary. Words that start with **Q, R, S, T, U, V, W, X, Y,** or **Z**, are found near the **back** part of the dictionary.

The last step to finding a word is to look at the **entry words**. The **entry words** are listed in the dictionary in alphabetical order, or alphabetized.

When trying to alphabetize words on your own, look at the first letter of each word. Let's look at the words below:

dog

cat

mule

goat

Notice that the first letter of dog is a **d**. The first letter in the next word cat is a **c**. Turn back to the alphabet section of this text. Which letter comes first in the alphabet? Of course **c** does. This means that the word **cat** comes before the word **dog** when alphabetized. So far, our alphabetized list looks like this since we just determined that the word **cat** comes before **dog**:

Does the **c** in **cat** come before the **m** in **mule** and the **g** in goat? Yes, it does. Now we know that the word **cat** is in the correct place within the list.

Original list	Alphabetical list
dog	c̲at
c̶a̶t̶	_____
mule	_____
goat	_____

Let's now go to the next word **dog**. Does the **d** in **dog** come before the first letter **m** in **mule** and **g** in **goat**? Yes, it does. Now we know that **dog** is currently placed in the correct position in the list.

Original list	Alphabetical list
d̶o̶g̶	c̲at
c̶a̶t̶	d̲og
mule	_____
goat	_____

Now that we know **cat** and **dog** are in the correct positions within the list, let's move to the next word.

Does the **m** in **mule** come before the **g** in **goat**? No, it does not. This means that these two words must be switched.

Is the list now in alphabetical order? Does the letter **d** come after the letter **c**? Yes. Does the letter **g** come after the letter **d**? Yes. Does the letter **m** come after the letter **g**? Yes. In this case our list is now in alphabetical order and looks like this:

Original list	Alphabetical list
~~dog~~	<u>c</u>at
~~cat~~	<u>d</u>og
~~mule~~	<u>g</u>oat
~~goat~~	<u>m</u>ule